ON THE COVER:

LIME AND COCONUT

A ornamental pineapple (*Ananus lucidus*)
B peperomia (*Peperomia caperata*)
C peperomia (*Peperomia* 'Bianco Verde')
D pink earth star (*Cryptanthus* 'Pink Star')
E ivy plants (*Hedera helix*)

First published in 2014 by Cool Springs Press, an imprint of the Quayside Publishing Group, 400 First Avenue North, Suite 400, Minneapolis, MN 55401

Cool Springs Press titles are also available at discounts in bulk quantity for industrial or sales-promotional use. For details write to Special Sales Manager at Cool Springs Press, 400 First Avenue North, Suite 400, Minneapolis, MN 55401 USA. To find out more about our books, visit us online at www.coolspringspress.com.

Library of Congress Cataloging-in-Publication Data

Asbell, Steve, 1983-
  Plant by numbers : 50 houseplant combinations to decorate your space / Steve Asbell.
     p. cm.
  50 houseplant combinations to decorate your space
  Includes index.
  ISBN 978-1-59186-549-0 (sc)
  1. House plants. 2. Indoor gardening. I. Title. II. Title: 50 houseplant combinations to decorate your space.

  SB419.A695 2014
  635.9'65--dc23

                    2013039019

Acquisitions Editor: Billie Brownell
Design Manager: Brad Springer
Layout: Diana Boger
Front Cover Design: Mary Ann Smith

Photo credits: page 12 (left): Katie Elzer-Peters, page 13: Shutterstock, page 38: Quayside Publishing Group, page 40 (top): iStock, page 40 (bottom): Lynn Steiner

Printed in China
10 9 8 7 6 5 4 3 2 1

PLANT BY NUMBERS

50 HOUSEPLANT COMBINATIONS TO DECORATE YOUR SPACE

STEVE ASBELL

COOL
SPRINGS
PRESS
Home and Garden Experts™

MINNEAPOLIS, MINNESOTA

DEDICATION

Nancy Asbell (1962–2012)
Artist, teacher, beacon of light.

I became a gardener several years ago just to give my handicapped mother a better view from her windows, so I suppose that if anything, it was her encouragement, remarkable attitude, and a shared love of nature that have made all of this possible.

Yet as I write this dedication, I realize that it has been exactly one year since my mother passed away from complications of lupus. The disease ravaged her body and left her handicapped and ridden with constant pain, yet even through her many brushes with death she was rarely seen without a beaming smile. In her private journals she often went so far as to thank God for her horrible illness, for the disease that had been tearing her apart since I was a child. In her final months she thanked God for the worst pain she had ever felt, just because she could then tell another sufferer, "I understand what you're going through." She thanked God for her beautiful tragedy because it enabled her to reach out to thousands of people and give them hope in their darkest hour, from her piano students to the strangers she reached out to on Facebook, urging them to "celebrate the day." She kept a gratitude journal called "Grace Notes" on her blog and Facebook, praying for strength "to be a beacon of light to others, to be a blessing, to be an encourager." She was immobile, racked with pain, and flat broke. At fifty years of age she was living the remainder of her life in a nursing home, yet

when she wrote her final "Grace Notes" with a weak and shaky hand, she had all of this for which she could give thanks: "Finding joy in all situations. Remembering my son and Jennifer's wedding. Starting at the bottom and working towards the top. Time with my sister Michelle. Clippings from the garden in small plastic bags so that I can smell and enjoy them. Missing my Facebook friends but knowing they are there for me. Being loved."

ACKNOWLEDGMENTS

It took a lot more than just words and pretty pictures to make this book. Since I designed and planted each of these container recipes by hand, it required several hundred plants, more than fifty containers, growing lights, potting soil, and places to shoot the arrangements as well. I'd like to thank Chris Trad and the staff at Trad's Garden Center for allowing me to use their plants, pots, and workspace; Nancy MacDonald for providing me her plants and valuable knowledge; Shawn Winchester and Karen Ryder for graciously letting me into their homes for photoshoots; and the vendors who saw potential in my book and provided their products: Sun-Gro, Bright Green, Sunlight Supply, Proven Selections, Native Cast, Fiskars, EZ-Mount Plant Hangers, Stewart's Greenhouse, and Central Florida Ferns. I couldn't have done any of this without your help! I'd also like to thank my two favorite container garden artisans—Kris Blevons and Candice Suter—for sharing photos of their arrangements. This book took a lot of help in the form of advice, patience, and emotional support. In no particular order, thank you to my family, Debra Lee Baldwin, Mr. Subjunctive, DGS, Billie Brownell (my amazing editor), Kylee Baumle, Jenny Peterson, Chad Davis, Jo and my neighbors, my coworkers and managers at my job, and my many wonderful Facebook friends who turned out to be so much more.

To my little sister Shannon Harper: You've always loved me unconditionally and Mom would be so proud of your grace and accomplishments. And to my dad, thank you for encouraging me to chase lizards and read books about nature as a kid. The other day I caught a lizard and then finished writing my own book for my own kid to read someday.

Most of all, I'd like to thank my patient wife, Jennifer, who watched our clean and peaceful home turn into a jungle-like indoor nursery and still gave me her unyielding support and assistance . . . even though I became too busy to cook her any meals. Or make the bed. Or put away my toys. She's my best friend and my one true love.

CONTENTS

INTRODUCTION

Can you think of a better place to garden than in the comfort of your own home? Whether you have a garden of your own or live in a tiny apartment, there are so many reasons to combine houseplants to create indoor gardens. First of all, it's a lot easier than you'd think. Instead of tending to a bunch of different potted plants around the house and inevitably forgetting to water one every now and then, combining them in one pot means you only have to water once. They're also a heck of a lot of fun to make. Even the most reluctant creative person would find it a lot easier to make a living arrangement of plants that already look beautiful on their own, and it's a lot less intimidating than painting or cooking. Best of all, indoor gardens give you a chance to design a garden for your bedroom or office even if you have no experience at all. A living arrangement of plants is as easy as making a flower arrangement, but it will last a whole lot longer.

YES, YOU *CAN* COMBINE HOUSEPLANTS

So why aren't more people doing it? It might be because they're afraid of failure. While plenty of books exist on so-called "mixed-plantings" and "container combinations" outdoors, with many of them even using plants that can be grown as houseplants, nobody seems to know which plants actually work together *indoors*. You've never had much luck with dish gardens (more on those later) or the readymade combinations at the garden center, so why risk putting your cherished houseplants together on your own if there's even the slightest chance that you'll be branded a "black thumb" or a "plant murderer"? After all, if the professionals can't pull it off, how should you? Well, the good news is that with the help of this book, you'll actually be better at artfully combining houseplants than your local florist. Well, unless she has a copy of this book herself.

Combine plants for a colorful, interesting look.

DISH GARDENS DONE RIGHT

Raise your hand if you've ever had a dish garden—you know, one of those bowls filled with cacti, ferns, or other houseplants. If so, raise your hand again if you've actually managed to keep it looking good for more than a year, and if you're one of the unlikely few geniuses who've accomplished this feat, set this book down and use your other hand to pat yourself on the back. But if you're a part of the majority who think themselves to be unfit to be gardeners, join the crowd and rest assured that it's not you; it's the dish garden.

Dish gardens are quite an impossible proposition: shallow bowls with no drainage holes consisting of tiny houseplants with totally different requirements (cactus and ferns, anyone?) that will either die or outgrow one another within a few months. Because dish gardens have no drainage holes, water collects and stagnates, rotting the roots and killing the plants. If you place the dish in the sun, the shade-loving plants burn and die off. If you keep it in the shade, the sun-loving plants stretch out and become weak, also eventually dying off. Those that are lucky enough to survive such treatment will eventually take over the bowl and either get repotted or die. If all of this seems a tad depressing, rest assured that it's an entirely different story if you use the right plants.

Using the right plants is the key to keeping a dish garden healthy.

HOUSEPLANTS MADE EASY

With the right combinations, growing houseplants together is actually easier than growing them separately. I first started combining my houseplants because I was too lazy and forgetful to keep up with watering each and every little potted plant in my collection, and I found that watering one big pot of houseplants was a whole lot easier. Because the pots have more room for potting mix, the plants have more room to grow the deep roots that help them grow stronger and endure more neglect. Less mess, less fuss, and less space make indoor gardening a lot more enjoyable, all the while looking even more like a real garden.

GROW A GARDEN *ANYWHERE*

You don't need an outdoor garden to create a lush and inviting paradise, and even the smallest indoor garden on your desk serves as a refreshing diversion from the rigors of everyday life. Trimming errant stems and dusting the leaves is a lot more relaxing than slaving away in a full-sized yard. When larger containers are grouped together, they become an even more realistic interpretation of the outdoors and can even be used to bridge together views from the world outside your window.

CREATE LIVING ART

Whoever said "art is dead" was dead wrong. Container combinations are works of living art that can be displayed almost anywhere in the home. You have a huge palette of colorful plants with patterns, textures, and shapes that almost seem as if they were already painted themselves, but what really makes painting with plants exciting is having the opportunity to work with a growing and changing medium. Vines ramble, bushes branch out, and dracaenas climb upwards toward the sky. As a garden artist you are drawing out the framework for a painting that paints itself.

You don't even need a shelf to grow a container garden.

It's not hard to have fun with your container gardens.

NERDY PLANT TERMS

If plant tags and instructions confuse you as much as they baffled me when I started gardening, maybe this section will help. Mark this page so that you can use it as a reference whenever you see a term that makes you scratch your head. If your head is still itchy even then, consider using a medicated shampoo.

POTTING

- **Potting Mix**— A soil-less replacement for garden soil that is used for indoor growing.
- **Drainage**— The ability of water to drain away from the roots.
- **Moisture Retentive**— The ability of potting mix to retain water like a sponge.
- **Aeration**— The ability of air to flow freely through the potting mix.
- **Amend**— To add other ingredients to the potting mix. This can increase drainage, moisture retention, and so forth.

An echeveria is an example of a rosette form.

Fittonia is a plant with variegated leaves.

PLANT ANATOMY

- **Foliage**—The leaves and stems of a plant.
- **Inflorescence**—A stem holding multiple flowers.
- **Crown**—Where the plant meets the soil.
- **Leaf Node**—Where the leaf meets the stem.
- **Rosette**—Leaves arranged tightly in a spiral.
- **Spathe**—The "sail" on the flower structures of peace lilies and anthuriums.
- **Variegated**—When leaves are patterned with another color.

PLANT NAMES

Plants have names, just like people. It's how we can distinguish one plant from another, especially when they have the same or very similar common names. And, common names vary across the country. So the "binomial nomenclature" system was developed to identify every living thing (plants and animals) by its genus and species name, as well as its common names.

- **Common Name**—(Example: rubber tree)
The "normal" name for a plant, a common name seems useful enough, at least until you realize that a lot of houseplants all respond to the same name, such as wandering Jew, palm tree, or Steve.

- **Scientific Name**—(Example: *Ficus elastica*)
While the scientific (or Latin) name can seem a bit cumbersome, it's the only way to describe a plant without confusing it with another plant by the same common name. It's appropriate that it's known as the Latin name because it's usually italicized, and it usually consists of a genus and a species.

- **Genus**—(Example: *Ficus*)
A genus is like a street gang from *West Side Story*. They're united by their obvious similarities, so they are often lumped in together. It's a lot easier to describe "Tony the *Ficus elastica*" as "Tony the Ficus" because you know that most ficus houseplants have the same requirements.

- **Species**—(Example: *elastica*)
Sometimes plants like Tony the Ficus need to stand apart from the crowd so they can start a family with someone from another genus. After all, Tony the *Ficus elastica* seems to have the hots for "Maria the *Schefflera actinophylla*" . . . even though that relationship is doomed on so many levels.

- **Cultivar**—(example: 'Tricolor')
A cultivar is a species that stands apart from the rest and gets its own name. As it turns out, Tony the *Ficus elastica* is even better at snapping his fingers than the rest and is also a snazzy dresser. Henceforth he shall be known as Tony the *Ficus elastica* 'Tricolor'.

Rubber tree, *Ficus elastic*

Texture—*How small the leaves look, fine being the smallest and coarse being the largest.*

Contrast—*When colors or textures of neighboring plants are drastically different. This creates impact.*

Repetition—*Repeating plants or visual qualities in an arrangement to make it look more pleasing.*

Harmony—*When neighboring plants are of similar color, form, and so forth. This makes compositions peaceful.*

Focal Point—*The largest and most prominent plant in a grouping, usually of a contrasting color or texture.*

THE ENVIRONMENT

LIGHT

The very first thing you should do when creating a container combo is decide where in the house it will be placed, and light is without a doubt the biggest factor. Before you skim over this chapter to get to the good stuff, you might want to take some time to get acquainted with the secret ingredient that will make or break your indoor container garden recipes.

You see, low light is the silent killer of houseplants. Light provides plants with the energy to grow and live, so expecting a ficus to live in the dark for a year would be a lot like trying to use a phone without a cord or charge. The most popular houseplants are so successful because they have adapted to life on the shadowy rainforest floor and can cope with the dark conditions in our homes. On the other hand, many houseplants such as succulents require intense light to thrive.

A room might seem bright enough to grow houseplants once you've flipped on the overhead lights or your eyes have adjusted to the shade, but plants usually need more light than we need to go about our daily business, and they also need it all day.

HOW MUCH LIGHT DO I HAVE?

No Light means that you cannot read at all without the aid of a light, and unfortunately it also means no houseplants. Rooms with no light include those without windows or those in which the blinds stay closed at all times. You can temporarily display arrangements in rooms without regular light if you're entertaining but not for long.

Low Light is bright enough to easily read a book without flipping on the light switch, yet only a handful of houseplants will actually survive in low light. Plants that can live in low light are usually deep green and include cast iron plant, snake plant, parlor palm, and ZZ plant. Low light is the low-life of the light levels and a real dimwit, and can be found asking "Got a light?" in shady

Bright light is the best lighting situation for most houseplants.

Succulents and cacti often prefer the sunny light of a south-facing window.

corners. It is tolerated by only the most patient plants, but it's never really enjoyed.

Bright Light receives no direct rays of light, yet it is bright enough to read a book without assistance. This is also known as medium light, bright indirect light, or filtered light, and it is the best lighting situation for most houseplants. A spot with bright light might be near a north-facing window, in a room with west- or east-facing windows, or at the back of a room with south-facing windows. Bright light is just perfect for most foliage plants because they don't like to get too extreme. Here they get plenty of light, yet not so much that they get sunburned.

Sunny Light is intense and direct and is usually found near a south-facing window where a distinctive ray of light is cast. Succulents, cacti, and prolific bloomers like lantana and bottlebrush will thrive here. Some of the plants in this book might prefer direct sunny light but may have been grown in bright indirect light before they were purchased. When moving new plants to direct sunlight, do it slowly so that the leaves do not scorch.

COPING WITH LOW LIGHT

While it might be true that people who live in glass houses shouldn't throw bricks, they probably should start growing houseplants. But not everyone is blessed with a bounty of windows, and you might find that your own windows are shaded by nearby buildings or trees. Before you decide to solve your lighting problem by breaking out the sledgehammer and installing new windows, try these tricks instead.

- **Move furniture** that may be blocking the windows.
- **Clean windows** to remove dirt and residue.
- **Trim trees** and bushes outdoors. Hire an arborist for bigger trees.
- **Move plants** to a brighter room, avoiding direct sunlight.
- **Choose plants** that are already tolerant of low light.
- **Install lighting** from one of the vendors listed on page 170.

HUMIDITY

Have you ever given your houseplant the perfect combination of light, water, and care just to watch it die for no good reason? It could be that it isn't getting enough humidity. Humidity is defined as the amount of moisture in the air, and some plants can't live without it. Even though it's the secret ingredient that some of the most exciting houseplants need to thrive, many plant labels still fail to mention a plant's humidity needs.

You can use a terrarium to increase the amount of humidity your plants receive.

Homes are at their driest in winter, when central heating robs the air of all moisture. Plants that need humidity include spikemosses, *Anthurium, Fittonia,* and most ferns, but the majority of houseplants will also perform better with humid air. You can provide humidity by doing one of several things.

- **Mist leaves** with a pump spray. Tank sprayers are easy and affordable.
- **Kitchens and bathrooms** are often more humid because of evaporating water.
- **Use a humidifier.** They can be found at drugstores and can hide behind your container planting.
- **Use a fountain.** A decorative tabletop water feature placed nearby adds humidity with style.
- **Combine humidity lovers** for easy misting or relocating.
- **Terracotta pots,** when moist, produce humid air in their vicinity.
- **Bring plants outside** to a shady spot in summer to bask in the moist air.
- **A tray of pebbles** under or near a pot will create a damp atmosphere for nearby plants.

PETS AND CHILDREN

Every so often you'll see an article about how poinsettias or other houseplants are poisonous. Let's be honest here: Most houseplants are poisonous if they're eaten in any large quantity, but so are many of the plants growing on the way to school or around the playground. A much more likely problem is the threat of them knocking over pots. Large and heavy ceramic, stoneware, and terracotta urns on the floor should stay put if they aren't too narrow at the base, but it's best to use soft and lightweight containers on tall surfaces so they don't fall and cause injury when the furniture gets bumped.

SPACE

You might be smitten with one of the larger container combinations in this book, but before you make your own, make sure you'll be able to get it in the car and up the stairs to a place that gives it plenty of room to be seen from a distance. Bear in mind that a full-grown container arrangement will be larger than a newly planted one. Also consider the weight. If you're not sure that your antique dresser can support a large combo in a heavy glazed urn, consider using a lighter container material or a smaller arrangement.

A large display like this makes a big impact, but only if you have the space.

TEMPERATURE

Temperatures can vary greatly indoors, and "room temperature" is never a guarantee. Some plants need cooler conditions in winter, and others require constant warmth, so I have made a note of these on page 61. Anyone who's lived in the South can attest that there's a difference between dry heat and humid heat. Desert plants prefer the former, and rainforest plants usually prefer the latter. Temperate houseplants like camellias and ivies despise the warm and dry air, so keep them in a well air-conditioned room in summer and move them to an unheated space in winter. Holiday cactus and other plants will survive through warm winters but bloom best if they experience a bit of cold temperatures above freezing.

VENTILATION

Good air movement is often overlooked as a requirement for growing houseplants, but it can be necessary to prevent diseases, pests, and other problems that proliferate in its absence. In mixed plantings, such as the ones in this book, the plants are even closer together and need ventilation even more. A small fan is an excellent remedy to stagnant air, as it doesn't take much to get air moving around a room.

HOW TO DESIGN A CONTAINER GARDEN

First, there is no wrong way when it comes to design. Planting a container garden recipe is just as easy as packing a suitcase. You start by making a list of things you want to pack, and then you pack all of your best clothes, entertainment, and necessities into a sturdy suitcase. With that analogy in mind, just close your eyes and take deep breaths. Plants will die, colors will clash, and you're definitely going to forget to water on occasion, but I'm here to tell you that as long as you realize that you cannot fail, everything is going to be *just fine*. Besides, plants already look good on their own, so it's pretty hard to make a truly ugly container garden.

GET INSPIRED!

I want you to do me a favor: Grab a sheet of paper and a pen for an anti-homework assignment in which your whole page will consist of daydreams and doodles. Fill that entire page with the things that you find beautiful, seeking inspiration from hobbies, colors, plants, fashion, cooking, and even advertisements. Define your goal, and the ingredients will magically fall into place. For a more direct route, just start with the plants themselves.

SET UP YOUR WORKSPACE

A cook needs a kitchen, and an artist needs a place to call her studio. Indoor gardeners just need a small place to plant their designs, be it in your home or outdoors on a patio or balcony. If you have the space, set aside an area to grow an entire palette of houseplants to use in your arrangements. If you don't have too many windows, consider purchasing a grow light. Your plants will grow more evenly if they're not all reaching for a window, and you can also use your light to grow vegetables when you're low on your "art supplies." I made my own space by purchasing an automotive drip pan and setting it on two crates. If you will be planting the containers indoors, use a water resistant tarp or plastic sheeting (both can be found at the hardware store) to keep your floor free of dirt.

An entire palette of houseplants can be an impressive sight.

GO SHOPPING

Now it's time for the fun part: plant shopping! There are a few ways to go about this. Larger retailers often have a good selection of houseplants, but because they don't receive the attention of a small and devoted staff, it's best to purchase plants that have just arrived on a shipment that haven't yet been overwatered or placed in the searing sun. On the other hand, they do have good return policies. Garden centers are awesome because both the plants and shoppers get special attention from a more experienced staff. When all else fails, you can order just about anything online nowadays, and there are several websites listed on page 170.

Individuals can shop from the retail nurseries, and your garden center can order from the wholesale nurseries.

When choosing a plant, inspect it thoroughly for signs of pests (page 39.) or poor watering habits (page 33). It's bad enough to have a plant die on you by no fault of your own, but a diseased or pest-ridden plant can infest the other plants in your indoor garden.

START WITH A SINGLE PLANT

Sometimes a very special plant is all the inspiration you need, so why not use that as a springboard? Start off with a plant that's either easy to grow or just one that you think is really exciting, even if it's just something you already have lying around the house. Learn about the plant's needs and make sure that they're easy for you to provide. You can also use a favorite container as your first step, choosing plants that complement and contrast with its colors and textures. Now it's time to pick the plant's friends using the plant palette on page 42. If your peace lily likes moist soil and bright indirect light, then its common interests will help it get along in any crowd. But thugs like the common rubber tree (*Ficus decora*) have aggressive roots that would crowd out any companions that need their own root space.

COLOR OUTSIDE THE LINES

We've all seen those gaudy flowerbeds in which the gardener clearly decided to grab every one of the day-glo flowers at the nursery, then scattered the petunias and violets in a traffic wreck of color that's confusing enough to make your eyes twitch a little. Even *that* gardener would have a hard time messing up a design with houseplants. Even though some indoor plants have some wickedly intense flowers of their own, they never seem to overpower the color of their leaves. They're even known in the trade as foliage plants! A good rule of thumb is to do everything in moderation. If you're using a bright pink *Dracaena marginata* 'Colorama' in a planting, there's no need to add too many other plants with vivid colors like orange or purple. Instead, stick to a gentler color and showcase the intensely colorful striped leaves of the dracaena by pairing it with leaves of light green, black, or sage.

GET A FEEL FOR TEXTURE

If you see me describing plants as "fine" or "unkempt and coarse" it might sound like I'm just making an observation on the plants' manners. I'm actually referring to texture or the appearance of their leaves from a distance. Maybe there's a correlation between leaf size and good manners after all, though, because a plant with small leaves is more likely to politely stay put and won't need much in the way of pruning. A plant with coarse leaves, on the other hand, can easily butt in and cover up smaller plants in your arrangements. If you need a plant that won't get in the way of its neighbors, look for the ones with small or narrow leaves. These provide a textural element that comes across as a bit of a surprise in the indoor landscape, and they offer a relief to the coarse foliage so typical of houseplants. Brash and bold plants with coarse foliage still have their place though, and it's usually somewhere in the center of attention. *Dracaena* and *Aglaonema* plants are perfect examples, erupting from the center of plantings with all the swagger of a well-paid rapper.

MAKING IT A HABIT

A plant's habit is best described as what it will do when it grows up, and its career path makes a big difference in how it will work within the cramped confines of a container planting. Case in point: You see a cute little salmon-colored plant at the garden center and decide to use three of them in a container planting. Within just a couple years, the *Syngonium* (you did read the label, right?) plants will ditch the petite pink look to become robust vines with enormous, green divided leaves. In Florida they can even reach the treetops if left unchecked! This isn't to say that it's a *bad* choice for a container combo, just as long as you know what to expect. Here is a list of different habits and uses, and how they can be used.

- **Creeping**—Spreads horizontally over the ground, sometimes spilling over the edge of the container.
- **Vining**—Fast-growing weak stems that use tendrils and other means for support. Smaller vines are preferable to large ones.
- **Clumping**—Forms new offsets at the base, forming a dense mound. These are versatile and keep within bounds.
- **Upright**—Grows vertically on one or more sturdy stems.
- **Bushy**—Produces a "bush" of densely packed stems. These make great fillers and can be pruned periodically to taste.

Keep the eventual sizes of the plants in mind. This combination planting of ti plant and macho fern might have looked cute at first, but now they're enormous!

- **Stoloniferous**—Rosettes of packed leaves grow on stems, useful for planting at the edge of containers. Examples include bromeliads like *Neoregelia* or succulents like *Echeveria*.
- If you're not sure about a plant's habit, check out the plant list beginning on page 53.

Combine light and dark plants to create interesting contrast.

THE VALUE OF GOOD CONTRAST

To create an attention-grabbing display, use contrast. Contrasting colors sit across from each other on the color wheel, and really stand out when combined in different values. A color's "value" is defined as its darkness or lightness, ranging from black to white. For example, a dark red bromeliad flower against an equally dark backdrop of green *Dracaena* 'Janet Craig' can appear unsettling, much like bright red words are difficult to read against a bright green background. To fix this, change the value of one of the colors and display the red bromeliad flower against the lighter lime green leaves of a *Dracaena* 'Limelight' instead.

LOCATION IS *EVERYTHING*

You wouldn't display a painting out of view of guests or yourself, so you certainly don't want to be shy about displaying your living creation. While accommodating the plant's needs with proper light is the priority, make sure you also put it in the spotlight where it can be enjoyed by you and your friends on a regular basis. Surround your design with a blank wall, display it in the center of a room, or make it the focal point of a large window. You'll grow to love your arrangements so much that you might even find yourself picking curtains and furniture to complement the colors of your dracaena. But they don't need to stay in one place. If you're entertaining friends or family in a dim room, arrangements can be moved out of the light for the evening and moved back the next day.

Oh, and just because these are houseplants doesn't mean they need to be confined to the house. Bring them to a shady patio or entryway outside in summer (or for warmer regions, whenever nights aren't frosty) so that they can liven up your garden and benefit from the brighter light, better ventilation, and more humid air (assuming you live where there is some outside humidity).

POTTING UP

You can use a standard potting mix or choose one that's custom made for your houseplants. A good potting mix provides plenty of breathing room for the roots, a starting dosage of nutrients, and moisture retention. Don't use garden soil for your houseplants, as it will suffocate the roots and kill your plants before you can even say "moisture retentive."

The potting medium is important enough when growing plants singly, but it's even more important in group plantings because it has to accommodate every plant in the container.

POTTING MIXES

- **Regular Mix**—If you're not sure which soil to use, regular potting mix is the "one size fits all" growing medium because it retains moisture well, yet still drains adequately enough to keep most houseplants' roots from rotting.
- **Moisture Retentive**—For plants that require constantly wet soil, choose moisture retentive potting mix. Ingredients like coir, peat moss, or gels help the mix stay moist for longer periods.
- **Cactus Mix**—There won't be many cacti in this book, but cactus mix is great for succulents, bromeliads, and other plants that hate wet feet. Water drains freely through the medium without stagnating.
- **Orchid Mix**—Usually made up of a mixture of bark, perlite, charcoal, and other amendments, orchid mix has the breathability and coarseness that orchids and other epiphytes love. Use it for epiphyte groupings or add it around the root zone of epiphytes planted with other houseplants.

Cactus mix allows water to drain freely.

AMENDMENTS AND ADDITIONS

For better control over your plants' growing conditions, you can mix in amendments. Depending on which one you use, they can improve drainage, change the soil's acidity, or retain moisture.

- **Vermiculite**—Made from the common mineral mica, vermiculite helps add aeration and drainage to potting mixes, yet holds enough moisture that it can be used on its own to start seeds and cuttings.
- **Perlite**—Helps water drain more quickly. Add this lightweight volcanic material to regular potting mix on a one-to-one ratio to grow succulents, and in a one-to-four ratio for plants that require both moisture and drainage.
- **Peat moss**—This is the main component of potting mixes and can be added whenever extra moisture retention or acidity is needed. It is not a renewable resource, but coir is a suitable replacement.
- **Coir**—This coconut palm product is a good alternative to peat moss, as it holds moisture quite well.
- **Sphagnum moss**—Used in place of potting mix for orchids and other epiphytes. Can be used to line planted wreaths or mounted arrangements. Choose long-grain moss for epiphytes and short-grain moss for propagating.
- **Orchid bark**—Bark harvested from fir trees that is used to grow orchids. This is a superior replacement for sphagnum moss for most orchids (with the exception of *Phalaenopsis*), as it doesn't get too soggy.
- **Activated charcoal**—Lowers the acidity of potting mixes and prevents rot. Is usually added in small amounts to orchid potting mixes.

CONTAINERS

Containers set the standard for your container combo, so quality is key. The right pot gives the eye a place to rest called negative space, and if chosen carefully it maintains a balance with the chosen plantings through repetition of colors, textures, and patterns.

The right container will balance the combination of plants you have.

MATERIALS

- **Glazed ceramic**—These glossy and colorful fired pots are expensive but are very durable and attractive. They are also heavy and ideal for large floor plantings.
- **Terracotta**—They might just be clay pots, but they develop an attractive patina of minerals or moss over time. They are perfect for succulents and epiphytes, as they have good aeration.
- **Fiberglass**—Relatively new to the scene, fiberglass pots are lightweight and affordable like plastic pots but are made to look almost as nice as glazed ceramic pots.
- **Plastic**—Though not the most attractive containers, plastic pots still get the job done. That is, until they fade and crack in the sunlight. Fiberglass pots are a good replacement.

SIZES

- **Tall pots**—These possess a stately elegance and command attention, all while saving space and giving the roots plenty of room to grow. Because they draw attention to themselves, spend a little more for glazed pottery.
- **Wide pots**—These are great for recreating the look of a landscape when filled with textural low growing plants and are also at the perfect height to serve as centerpieces.
- **Small pots**—These can be just as impressive as big pots with the right design and placement. If you pick small plants, you can still create a thriving ecosystem on your desktop.

THINKING OUTSIDE THE CONTAINER

Driftwood can be a good basis for a container garden.

A few of the designs in this book break beyond the conventional definition of a container garden. The truth of the matter is that with the right plants, a living arrangement can be held together by nothing more than a lava rock, a chunk of tree fern trunk, a slab of bark, or even a branch of driftwood. Epiphytes and succulents can be easily mounted by taking cuttings (page 37), wrapping the cut end with sphagnum moss, and attaching them to the surface of your choice with twine or twist ties. To water plants mounted in this manner, just mist them occasionally, soaking the sphagnum moss and growing surface. Another way to grow plants without containers is to do this take on a traditional Japanese method called *Kokedama*. Just take a plant out of its pot, pack peat moss or coir tightly around the rootball, and then wrap it with sphagnum moss, using twine. Insert cuttings and place the *Kokedama* in a dish. Water it frequently enough that the rootball stays moist.

HOW TO PLANT A CONTAINER COMBO

The key to a successful container planting is in the, well, planting! Messing this part up can leave you with some sad-looking plants, but doing it right the first time means that they'll thrive from day one. Of course it helps if you start out with some cool tools like my Garfield trowel or Shawna Scoop, but I've planted many arrangements using nothing but an empty flowerpot for scooping and my hands for packing.

- **Plan ahead.** Choose plants that can grow in the same conditions, using the list on page 53 as a guide. Before purchasing the plants, play around with different arrangements to see how they would look together.
- **Prepare the soil and plants.** Water the plants *and* potting mix a few hours before planting. This will help the plants establish and ensure that the soil is moist and workable. If you're mixing your own potting mix using amendments, combine them now.
- **Add a layer of drainage.** Use packing peanuts, crumpled up plastic pots, or soda bottles to make a layer no deeper than one-fourth of the container's depth. This will help excess water drain through the hole at the base of the pot.
- **Add potting mix.** As you pour or scoop in potting mix, tamp it down lightly with your hands or a trowel. Otherwise the mix will sink and settle in after planting, leaving dry air pockets around the roots. An air pocket will make the roots dry out and die, weakening the plant.

You don't need a lot of fancy tools to plant a container garden.

- **Remove plants from their pots.** Gently tease apart (separate) the roots of each plant so that they fan out. For rootbound plants, use a sharp knife to make two cuts through the bottom of the coiled mass of roots. Don't be afraid to do that. Place the unpotted plants aside on sheets of newspaper.
- **Arrange plants.** Place the potted plants atop the potting mix in the desired arrangement,

Adding decorative mulch can enhance your creation.

adding or removing potting mix so that the crown (where the soil meets the stem) of each plant rests within an inch of the container's rim. Smaller plants or cuttings can be tucked into the smaller openings between plants.

- **Fill the gaps.** Using a spoon or a small trowel (a kid-sized Garfield trowel is my favorite), fill in the gaps around each plant, gently pressing it down around the roots. Add more until the surface of the potting mix is level with the crowns of each plant. Do not let it settle against the crowns, as it can promote rotting.

- **Add decorative elements.** If you're using a decorative mulch such as sand or bark, add it now. Certain combinations (especially those with succulents) can be improved with the addition of little knick-knacks like seashells, marbles, or figurines. Don't worry about it looking too tacky; just have fun!

There, wasn't that fun? Let's do another one.

CARE

A recipe for baking cookies is pretty useless if you don't already know how to use an oven. Each container garden "recipe" in this book has its own unique instructions that will tell you almost everything you need to know about keeping the selected plants happy. The recipes are enough to get you started, but this chapter will give you the knowledge to improvise when you choose to make your own combinations, or even if you just need a Plan B when one of your plants begins the countdown to self-destruct.

SECRETS OF A GREEN THUMB

Just as babies don't come into the world with an inherent knack for brain surgery, nobody pops out of the womb with green thumbs intact. Maybe you had yellow thumbs like me, but that was just the jaundice.

Whenever people learn that I'm a garden writer, they invariably tell me about their attempts at keeping plants alive and ask me how I do it. I then ask, "Well, what plant is it?" and they give a response like "an orchid" or "vegetables" and eagerly await my response. I eventually figure out the identity of the plant and tell them how it should be grown. The point is that how you care for a plant depends entirely on the specific plant in question. A cactus from the desert has completely different requirements than those of a nerve plant or a peace lily.

This planting is so easy to make and grow—I just planted cuttings and watered it once every one to three weeks.

LEARN ABOUT YOUR PLANTS

Researching a plant is so crucial yet doing so can be so fast. It could be as simple as looking at the instructions on the plant's tag or asking a garden center employee for help, but those instructions are sometimes wrong or lacking in detail. Better yet, look the plant up online or in a book so that you know how to keep it alive. Got a mobile device? Just do a quick search right then and there! The

Be sure you know what you're growing and what the needs for each individual plant are.

Resources section on page 170 lists websites that will aid you in your search, and the plant directory on page 53 lists many of the versatile plants used in this book.

LISTEN TO YOUR PLANTS

The second secret to growing healthy plants is the same as the secret to growing healthy relationships: You have to be a good listener. Tragically, plants have all the social skills of wallflowers, so you'll never hear a bellowing "Feed me, Seymour!" from your hungry houseplant. That's because plants are infamous for keeping their non-existent mouths shut when they're unhappy and instead prefer to use the botanical equivalent of sign language to get their point across.

A good listener would pick up on visual cues like yellowing leaves and respond by thoughtfully serving up a helping of bone meal with a side of compost tea. This and other cries for help (dropping leaves, scabby growths, pest infestations) should be addressed by following the tips on page 39.

Sometimes you'll wonder if it's just better to put the poor thing out of its misery, and that's okay. If all the king's horses and all the king's men couldn't possibly put your houseplant back together again, don't be afraid to dump it like a bad egg. A dying plant could easily spread pests and diseases to its neighbors in the same container or in the same room, so there's no glory in fighting until the end. This leads us to the next macabre step.

KILL YOUR PLANTS

What? Now before you knock your begonia off the windowsill, realize that your plants will eventually die thanks to mistakes of your own doing. My point is that you shouldn't beat yourself up about it.

A frustrated gentleman once told me that he would grow plants but could never seem to keep vegetables like tomatoes alive for more than a year and felt like a failure. You can imagine his relief when I told him that tomatoes have to be replanted yearly anyway. Every plant killed brings you one step closer to the enlightened ranks of green thumbs because you begin to accept the comings and goings of nature and the inevitability of death and suffering. The other lesson is less profound: Every time you kill a plant, you learn a new way to keep the next one alive.

WATERING

How often you should water depends on a lot of variables, so I'm treating each container recipe on a case-by-case basis, giving each its own watering instructions. If you plan on making your own combinations though, here are some guidelines.

Selaginella needs high humidity and can be a challenging plant to grow, but the results are spectacular.

WHEN TO WATER

It's better to water your houseplant too little than too often because too much water promotes rot and decay, yet the first reaction to seeing a wilting overwatered plant is to water it even more. Because figuring out when to water seems to be the most confusing part of keeping houseplants for most people, let's just cut to the chase by breaking everything down into two lists: reasons to water less and reasons to water more.

Reasons and Signs to Water More

- Drooping leaves and stems.
- Lower leaves begin fading before dropping.
- Leaves look dull when they normally look glossy.
- Soil is so dry that it has shrunk, leaving a gap against the container.
- Roots are brittle and shriveled looking.

- The plants included are moisture lovers. (See the list on page 61.)
- The potting mix is rock hard and lightly colored.
- Water runs right through the pot when watering.
- The container is small or shallow.
- Entire container combo is light.

Reasons and Signs to Water Less
- Soil is sopping wet and feels distinctly "muddy."
- Roots have rotted and become black or mushy.

- Plant easily detaches from the soil.
- Potting mix is black and wet looking.
- There is no drainage hole at the bottom of the pot.
- Water sits in the drainage saucer.
- There is an overall bad smell.
- The plant is a succulent or drought lover. (See list on page 64.)
- The container is tall—this means it can hold water longer.
- The entire container combo is heavy.

HOW TO WATER

In the classic movie *Breakfast at Tiffany's*, Audrey Hepburn's infamous character set a horrible example for young women in the 1960s with her utter disregard for the rules. No, I'm not talking about smoking cigarettes in questionable company, petty shoplifting, or any of her other quirks, but something far more reckless and dire. When Holly Golightly snuck into a stranger's house wearing nothing more than a robe, she flirtatiously approached the naked man in bed with a drink in hand and committed a most unthinkable sin: She tossed her alcoholic beverage on the hapless man's houseplant with a total disregard for its watering guidelines. There was surprisingly little public outcry at the debacle, but fortunately, slipping houseplants martinis never really caught on either.

So now that we've marked "martinis" off the list of ways *not* to water your plants, here's how to do it the right way.

- **Use a narrow spout** to water plants with precision. Only the soil needs to be watered, not the leaves and the table.
- **Water slowly and evenly** so that each plant's rootball is moistened. Water too quickly, and it will speed right past the roots.
- **Use a saucer** to catch extra water and keep surfaces dry. Unless you're growing thirsty plants (page 65) don't let the water sit in the saucer, as it will cause the roots to rot.
- **Use warm water** whenever possible as many houseplants are sensitive to cold water.
- **Avoid wetting leaves** on plants with fuzzy leaves, as it will likely lead to rotting.

FERTILIZING AND GROOMING

Just as gardening outdoors requires such tasks as pulling weeds and removing dead leaves, so does a healthy and attractive indoor garden. A layer of dust and a petticoat of dead leaves are more than just unattractive; they promote disease and make perfect hiding places for pests. Here are some ways to get your groom on.

You won't need big tools to prune your container garden.

GROOMING

- **Clean large leaves** with a damp rag, wiping from the stem outward on each side of the leaves.
- **Remove dead leaves** by hand or with a small pair of pruners. Also remove any dead flowers or stems.
- **Pull weeds** from the potting mix by hand, pulling from the base of each weed so that the roots are removed.
- **Hose off plants** outdoors periodically with a fine mist to dislodge pests and dust. Do this in the shade to avoid burning the foliage.

PRUNING

Refresh your container gardens with a light pruning from time to time. Here are some reasons to break out the pruning shears.

- **Remove yellowing foliage** with clean pruners to prevent the spread of disease.
- **Thin out plantings** by removing old or weak stems at the base.
- **Prune the stem tips** of bushy plants to maintain a full look.
- **Make more plants** by taking cuttings, following the directions on page 37.
- **Scale back tall plants** like ficus trees by removing the tallest stems.

Every indoor gardener needs a pair of pruners, and a small pair of clippers is just the right tool for most jobs. To remove larger, woody stems, use a pair of curved bypass pruners.

FERTILIZING

Houseplants are usually sold with fertilizer in their potting mix, but it will only last for a few months. They typically don't need as much fertilizer as plants grown outdoors, but they will still need regular applications of fertilizer to continue looking as healthy as they did when bought. Well-fed plants are also better equipped to fend off pests and diseases. Heavy bloomers need more fertilizer than other houseplants because it takes a lot of effort to keep putting out all of those flowers. If possible, give them a product with extra phosphorus to get even more blooms. Plants that need less fertilizer include cacti, most succulents, and ferns. In fact, a lot of succulents and bromeliads color up more nicely when starved, so to speak.

There are several different types of fertilizer, but because they all have different ingredients, each has its own instructions. There are types formulated specifically for cacti, orchids, even African violets! Whichever one you choose, a good rule of thumb is to avoid overfertilizing, especially when using synthetic fertilizers, as it damages the plant more than it helps. If the minerals have already built up to form a white or yellow crust on the pot, flush out the built up minerals by rinsing them out with a deep watering and clean the crusty material built up

Brewing your own compost tea can save money and keep your plants from getting too much fertilizer.

on the pot. My personal favorite is compost tea because you don't have to worry about using too much and harming the plant. You just brew it like tea and use it to water your plants as needed, with none of the complicated schedules required of synthetic products.

DIVIDING, REPLANTING, AND PROPAGATING

I'd like to tell you that plants live happily ever after when they pass away, but despite St. Peter's extensive vocabulary of botanical Latin, there are no pearly garden gates awaiting the arrival of your overwatered orchid. Just ditch the plant, shed some tears (in case anybody is watching), and move on.

Some plants, such as begonias, have a relatively short life compared to their neighbors in the container and might die back after one to two years. These temporary plants and other victims could be replaced in one of a few ways. They can be started via cuttings at any point in their life and planted as small transplants when they decline, replaced with entirely different plants, or, if the surrounding plants have filled in by then, you can just remove the dying plant and leave the spot empty.

For many plants, it's fairly easy to propagate new ones.

MAKING MORE HOUSEPLANTS

One of the most rewarding experiences in indoor gardening is making new plants for free with what you already have.

STEM CUTTINGS

Using sharp pruners, make a cut just above a bud or leaf node. Remove shorter lengths from small plants and longer stems from large plants. Some cuttings will root in a vase of water, but the best method is to lightly dust the cut tip with rooting hormone and insert it into a moist medium such as vermiculite or seed starting mix. Easy candidates for stem cuttings include pothos, dracaena, and mistletoe cactus.

AIR LAYERING

For some of the larger houseplants, air layering is the way to go. For woody plants like ficus trees, start by selecting a stem and making a notch with a sharp knife about a foot down from the growing tip. Remove any leaves from this area. Peel or scrape away a small patch of the surface where you made a notch and apply rooting hormone. Then tightly wrap moist sphaghnum moss around the patch with a plastic bag and seal it shut with a rubber band or twist ties. Other good plants for air layering include dumb cane, dracaena, and schefflera.

LEAF CUTTINGS

Snake plants, begonias, African violets, and many succulents can be started from leaf cuttings. This is done much like stem cuttings but with leaves. Some, such as echeverias, must be planted with the whole leaf intact with the cut end inserted into the soil. The leaves of snake plants can be cut into separate segments and inserted into the soil right side up. Many begonias will root along any part of the leaf and can be cut up into sections or rooted whole, planted with the underside facing down.

SEEDS

Starting houseplants from seed takes a lot longer, but few things are more rewarding than helping a plant grow from a microscopic seedling into a full grown palm tree or bromeliad. Each plant has different requirements for starting from seed, but generally speaking, seed starting mix or vermiculite are good growing mediums. The smallest seeds can be grown in a clear Tupperware container or any other sealed plastic tray.

Starting seeds is a rewarding way to get more plants for your arrangements.

DIVISION

Divide plants by removing them from the container grouping and, using a clean knife, slicing through the mass of stems and roots to break it up into segments. After dividing the plant, place one of the divisions back in the original container with fresh potting mix and plant the others up in new pots.

PROBLEM-SOLVING: PESTS AND DISEASES

Most problems with pests or diseases can easily be prevented with proper care and a keen eye, but if your plant is already suffering, follow these steps.

- **Inspect each plant** in the pot first, as there might be other pests weakening the plant of which you weren't already aware. Place the planter at eye level, in a brightly lit room away from other plants so that you can easily spot problems without infecting the rest of your collection. If you place the container on a white sheet of paper, you'll be able to spot any pests that fall.

- **Wipe the leaves** of each plant with a damp rag and look for anything out of the ordinary, such as sticky honeydew, spotty-looking dust, or hard "scales." The problem areas to watch are the oldest leaves, "ugly" leaves, the undersides of leaves, and the leaf axils—the point where the leaves meet the stem.

- **Check the roots** next by either gently sliding the plants out of their pot, or in the case of larger pots, by brushing away the soil surface with a trowel. If the roots fill the pot and leave little room for potting medium, then it is time to repot. If the roots are mushy and rotting, then you may be watering too much. Gently teasing the roots apart with your hands, remove the dead roots with a sharp clean knife, and place the plants in fresh soil.

- **Wash your hands** and tools after inspecting each plant so that you don't spread potential problems to other plants or container combinations. Now that you've inspected your plants,

- **Identify the pests** by referring to the handy guide that follows.

PESTS

Don't blame the pests for attacking your plants. They're just looking for an easy meal, and your neglected ficus has "wounded prey" written all over it. Just as humans can prevent a cold with a healthy lifestyle, a properly cared-for plant is likely to be pest free. Because the plants in these groupings are likely to be growing closely, you can treat pests better by thinning out congested areas with a vigorous pruning following the tips on page 35.

Scale insects are easily removed by scraping them with your fingernail.

- **Scale**—Noticed as crusty discs on the surfaces of stems and leaves. These are easily removed by hand, but treat heavy infestations by spraying with insecticidal soap or a solution of roughly 1 tablespoon of dish soap to gallon of water.

- **Mealybugs**—They're often noticed as tiny white fluffs of cotton candy on your favorite houseplant, and if there's one good thing to be said about this fluffy scale insect, it's that they're easy to spot and remove. Picking them off by hand is decidedly gross, yet effective. Spray large infestations with insecticidal soap.

- **Spider mites**—These microscopic spider relatives aren't usually noticed until the leaves start to turn yellow or dry out. If you run a damp paper towel over a leaf and find little red or brown specks, you have spider mites. Treat by lightly cleaning the leaves with a damp rag or a tank mister. Prevent spider mites by providing higher humidity or wiping the leaves regularly.

- **Thrips**—Occasionally thrips will leave little slash marks on the leaves of your houseplants. They look a lot like spider mites to the naked eye, only narrower. Treat by rinsing with water.

- **Fungus gnats**—If you start to notice little black gnats in your home, you likely have fungus gnats. They breed in the potting medium of chronically overwatered plantings, but you can catch adults with homemade traps of index cards swabbed with petroleum jelly, and treat severe infestations by watering with a product called *B.T.* (*Bacillus thuringiensis*) according to label instructions.

Spider mites are hard to see, but their damage is easy to spot.

I had a treefrog living in my house to eat bugs, but you might need to use other measures.

DISEASES

If one of the plants in a container combination is diseased, quarantine the plant by removing it from the planting, removing affected parts, and repotting in fresh potting mix. Once the plant is healthy, it can be added to the group planting again. Most diseases are caused by overwatering or poor air circulation, so ensure that the plant's neighbors are properly cared for.

- **Rot**—If you notice dark and mushy spots on the stems, roots, or crowns of your plants, they have been overwatered and are starting to rot. Remove affected portions with a sharp, clean knife and replant separately in fresh potting mix. If the rotting occurs at the crown, it's usually best to discard the plant and start over.

- **Virus**—If a plant has been growing slowly despite proper care and is only putting out streaked or stunted foliage, it may have a virus. Viruses are usually passed along between plants by pests or unclean pruning shears and are prevented by cleaning your tools and removing pests. Unfortunately, there is no way to cure virus-infected plants, so you must dispose of them promptly.

PLANT PALETTE

BROMELIADS

When people tell me that they can't keep houseplants alive, I tell them to grow bromeliads—particularly the tree-dwelling vase-forming ones. Watering is as easy as pouring water in the vase formed by their tightly sealed leaves, letting a little trickle down to the roots below. Because the roots of vase-type bromeliads exist primarily for attachment purposes, they are easy to transplant into rootbound groupings. Grow bromeliads in bright indirect light, with the exception of neoregelias, which color up best with some direct sun. Fertilize lightly with diluted orchid food or compost tea.

The most popular *Aechmea* bromeliad is the silver vase plant (*A. fasciata*) with its white powdered sage green leaves and long-lasting pink inflorescence, but there are many others from which to choose. The queen's tears plant (*Billbergia nutans*) and others in its genus are useful for their upright and muted rosettes but are usually grown for their dangling flowers that look much like those of fuchsias. Guzmanias are some of the most widely available bromeliads and are treasured for their long lasting bloom spikes and glossy green leaves. But don't stop there. The flowers of *Neoregelia* are often hidden deep in the vase, but the colors and patternings on their leaves are so bright and varied that you won't even notice. Some, such as *Neoregelia* 'Scarlet Charlotte', start changing to rich hues

Bromeliads are some of the easiest houseplants to grow.

before blooming, earning the name of "blushing bromeliad." Some *Vriesea,* such as the flaming sword (*Vriesea splendens*) have interestingly patterned foliage and bright red flower spikes in the shape of a feather. Others merely have green leaves but are worthwhile for their durability, versatility, and long-lasting blooms.

Earth stars (*Cryptanthus* spp.) are the most useful terrestrial bromeliads, as they make excellent groundcovers for container plantings grown away from direct sun. 'Pink Star' and 'Red Star' are two of the smaller hybrids and work well in smaller pots. Other terrestrial bromeliads for container plantings include ornamental pineapples (*Ananas*), *Orthophytum,* and *Dyckia*. They all tolerate drought but perform best with regular water.

BULBS

An unexpected blooming bulb adds a welcome element of surprise to container plantings, not unlike the appeal of an outdoor garden. Temperate bulbs such as daffodils, crocus, and hyacinths need cold temperatures in winter but can be forced into bloom by bringing them indoors in late winter. In warmer climates, store them in a refrigerator from fall through winter to trick them into blooming. Add them to container combinations, enjoy their flowers, and bring them back to the garden when they've finished blooming. Those in warm areas such as southern California and Florida should discard them afterward because they will not thrive in a hot climate.

Tropical bulbs, on the other hand, are perfect for growing indoors year-round. Most require a period of dormancy and will do best if water is withheld somewhat when the foliage begins to decline. Most of the tropical bulbs are not really bulbs at all, but rather fancy things called corms, rhizomes, and tubers. We'll just call them bulbs. Most of the tropical bulbs do best if they're given a cool rest period in winter in which the potting mix is allowed to dry out between watering. Amaryllis (*Hippeastrum*) bulbs are the most popular but are best grown alone because they need frequent repotting. Caladiums do produce interesting flowers when grown well, but they're mostly grown for their broad and intricately patterned colorful leaves. Lily of the Nile (*Agapanthus*) plants are treasured for the blue flowers that appear on tall stalks in spring. Rain lilies (*Zephyranthes*), blood lilies, and hurricane lilies (*Lycoris*) are also known as surprise lilies because they seem to bloom when you least expect it. Hurricane lilies are unique in that they go dormant in late spring and bloom in late fall on tall stalks. Clivias and crinums are quite large, so use them as a focal point in a large planting.

Calla lilies provide long-lasting blooms for cut-flower arrangements.

CACTI

Broadly speaking, there are two types of cacti: those that grow in the desert and those that grow in the treetops of tropical forests.

Even though **desert cacti** are a prickly proposition, they're certainly worthwhile for their feathery blooms or for designing an arrangement with a desert theme. Combine desert cacti with succulents in cactus potting mix and grow them in the direct sunshine of a south-facing window. Good desert cacti for interior arrangements include those in the genera of *Cereus* (monstrose forms), *Mammillaria, Gymnocalycium, Echinopsis,* and *Rebutia.* There are so many cacti from which to choose that many don't have common names or share them with entirely different plants. To remove overgrown cacti from their arrangement, cut into the potting mix around the plant with a sharp knife so that it will be easier to remove. Using gloves, wrap the cactus with strips of paper and gently lift the plant with a gloved hand, using your other hand to cut through any persistent roots.

The **forest cacti** are immensely more useful in mixed plantings because they usually lack spines, grow well without direct light, can be grown in moist soil as well as *without* soil—and did I mention they don't have spines? They are among the easiest plants to grow, can endure very long periods without water, and have recently become widely available at large retailers. Mistletoe cacti (*Rhipsalis*) produce leafless narrow green stems that hang down like spaghetti. Use these wherever a finely textured draping plant is needed. Holiday cacti (*Schlumbergera*) and Easter cacti (*Hatiora*) are the most familiar faces and produce the showiest blooms if given a cool rest period before their namesake holidays. Epiphyllums have broad flattened stems and are larger and coarser than the other plants, but serve well as centerpieces in larger plantings and produce blooms the size of dinner plates. Epiphytic forest cacti will be happy in just about any potting medium, from moist regular potting mix to orchid mix or even attached to a branch. They tolerate very low light but bloom and perform best in a bright room. They can even be included alongside succulents in a sunny planting, provided they're slowly moved to the sunny spot to avoid burned foliage.

DRACAENAS

Dracaenas are the undisputed king of houseplants and never fail to make a big impression as the centerpiece to your container designs. 'Janet Craig' dracaena (*Dracaena deremensis* 'Janet Craig') is popular, but its showy cultivars are especially useful. 'Limelight' has bright green leaves ranging from gold to chartreuse, and 'Warneckii' has white stripes on the margins of each sage green painted leaf. *Dracaena marginata* has deep green narrow leaves edged in red, but cultivars like 'Colorama' are so brightly colored with red and white that they appear to be pink. The corn plant (*Dracaena fragrans*) is unimpressive in its usual form, but some cultivars like *D. fragrans lindenii* appear to glow with a fountain of bold, golden chartreuse foliage. The plant commonly known as lucky bamboo is also a dracaena, and though it's normally sold as cuttings in water, *Dracaena sanderiana* does even better in potting mix. It's the perfect centerpiece for a small container planting and is even available in a variegated form! The black sheep of the group is *Dracaena godsffiana*, as it looks more like a shrub than the rest and has gold and cream splotches and dots rather than stripes.

The ti plant (*Cordyline fruticosa*) is an estranged relative of the dracaenas and needs a more humid environment than the rest, but the colorful leaves of cultivars like 'Red Sister' are so intense and unique that you'll find yourself buying a humidifier for the chance to grow a hot pink plant in your home.

'Limelight' dracaena brightens up dim rooms with bright foliage.

FERNS

Few plants have the soft and feathery appeal of ferns, and contrary to popular belief, not all are finicky. Bird's nest ferns (*Asplenium nidus* and so forth) lack the fine texture you would expect of a fern, but they make for dramatic and architectural focal points and are very resilient. Table ferns (*Pteris* spp.) are also quite durable and are notable for their airy silvery sage fronds. The most common ferns in the home are Boston ferns (*Nephrolepis* spp.), and they range from the lacy and delicate fronds of 'Fluffy Ruffles' to those of the imposing macho fern (*Nephrolepis biserrata*). These and several others will perform well with only average humidity, though an occasional misting improves their appearance greatly. Grow ferns in bright light, keeping them away from direct sunlight.

Maidenhair fern provides a delicate texture.

As you might expect, the frilliest ferns are the most delicate. Hare's foot fern (*Davallia canariensis*) and maidenhair fern (*Adiantum raddianum*) need moist air and constant moisture to survive. Spikemosses (*Selaginella* spp.) are fern relatives with densely arranged fronds that make them useful as groundcovers for terrariums or containers with other humidity-loving plants.

PALMS

No plant captures the feel of the balmy tropics better than a palm tree, and while some of the popular palms grow too large, many are well suited to container groupings. Of all of the palms available, chamaedoreas are the best for indoor growing. The parlor palm (*Chamaedorea elegans*) gets my vote for its smaller size, feathery deep green leaves, and tolerance of low light and neglect. They are usually sold as small containers of tiny seedlings and start off really small but can eventually grow several feet tall on narrow stems. Others include tuna tail palm (*C. metallica*) and the bamboo palms (*C. seifrizii, C. microspadix,* and *C. erumpens*). Use these as a centerpiece or as the backdrop to plants with brightly colored foliage. Lady palms (*Rhapis* spp.) are often expensive but are well worth it for the ambience they impart to Asian or tropical-themed plantings with their broad and glossy leaflets. Parlor palms (*Howea* spp.) are also tolerant of low light and make for impressive centerpieces in a traditional arrangement.

The palms listed in this book all require bright indirect light and a moist potting medium for the best growth. Remove the underground runners of clumping species (*Rhapis* spp., some *Chamaedorea* spp.) with a sharp knife if they begin to fill the pot.

PEPEROMIAS

If you have a houseplant with waxy leaves and have no clue as to its identity, it's probably a black pepper relative called a peperomia. These are some of the more versatile plants for container combinations, especially in smaller groupings where many of them can put their diverse sizes and forms to good use. There are three loosely defined groups with different habits: creeping, upright, and mounding. Creeping buttons (*Peperomia rotundifolia*) is one of the creeping species, and is a perfect addition to terrariums and extra small groupings. Other creeping peperomia cultivars and species include the bright green 'Isabella', 'Cupid', and *Peperomia glabella*.

Upright peperomias range from the bushy and big to the small and delicate. Baby rubber plant (*P. obtusifolia*) is one you've likely seen before, probably in its variegated form. Its 2-inch-wide leaves on busy stems make it a good filler in larger arrangements, and it can even be used as a focal point in the center of finer-textured plants. The tiny and upright 'Bianco Verde' has dark leaves on reddish-colored stems and provides nice contrast.

Mounding peperomias are popular for their dense clumps of ornately textured foliage, especially in the case of *Peperomia caperata* and its cultivars. 'Ripples' is one such plant, bearing round, rippled metallic leaves like waffle fries made of gunmetal. Watermelon plant (*P. argyaus*) is another shapeshifter in the genus with teardrop-shaped leaves patterned to resemble the outer rind of a watermelon.

Contrary to many of the books on houseplants, not all peperomias hail from the rainforest. Succulent varieties are especially fun because they have windows on the upper surface of their leaves, making them look as if they're made of jelly. Red peperomia (*P. graveolens*) has red undersides and clear windows on fat and succulent leaves. 'Peppy' has windows too, but the leaves are bright green and elongated, taking on the appearance of green beans.

PHILODENDRONS AND POTHOS

The philodendrons are best divided into two groups for the purposes of this book: vining and self-heading. For the most part, only one vining philodendron is suitable for combinations, because the others are just too big and rambunctious. Heart leaf philodendron (*Philodendron hederaceum*) is a very easy plant with small heart-shaped green leaves, and it even comes in cultivars like the velvety black 'Micans' and the golden chartreuse 'Aureum', making it very versatile for a number of color schemes. Self-heading philodendrons tend to stay put in one spot, forming a tight rosette of large and often colorful leaves. 'Black Cardinal' is grown for its glossy black leaves, 'Moonlight' is chartreuse, and 'Prince of Orange' produces new leaves in vivid

continued on page 48

orange, which turn green as they age. The split-leaf philodendrons (*Philodendron bipinnatifidum* and 'Xanadu') are impressive but too large and unwieldy for all but the largest groupings.

The pothos plants (*Epipremnum* and *Scindapsus*) are similar to the vining philodendrons but far more diverse and widely grown. They are usually distinguished from philodendrons by the tendency of their leaves to curve slightly to the side rather than symmetrically. The most common is the golden pothos (*Epipremnum aureum*) with its dappled gold and green leaves, but there are many more exciting cultivars, including the sage and white splashed 'Marble Queen' and the solid chartreuse 'Neon'. The satin pothos (*Scindapsus pictus* and *S. pictus argyraeus*) are cherished for their satin-textured shimmering sage leaves. The former has small, deep muted green leaves spotted with silver, and the latter has large quilted leaves of silver and sage.

BIG AND LEAFY PLANTS

The plants in this section all have a few things in common. They have large and lush tropical-looking leaves, grow well in moist soil, and require the bright indirect light that can be found in most of your home. Each of these plants can be combined together or combined with smaller moisture-loving plants like nerve plant (*Fittonia*), waffle plant (*Hemigraphis*), and ferns.

The plants in the *Maranta*, *Calathea*, and *Stromanthe* genera can be called prayer plants for their habit of folding up their leaves at night as if in prayer. Herringbone plant (*Maranta tricolor*) is the most popular, and its red-striped leaves are small enough to include as a filler plant in smaller arrangements. The narrow-leaved peacock plant (*Calathea lancifolia*) is one of the easiest in this group, as it tolerates neglect and low humidity more than the rest. Use this and taller prayer plants in the center or background of your plantings. The showier calatheas and stromanthes (*C. makoyana*, *Calathea crocata*, *S. sanguina*, and so forth) are definitely worth growing for their intense colors and patterns, but will need extra humidity. Provide this following the steps on page 18.

The gingers are similar to the prayer plants in that they have ornately patterned foliage and love moist soil and humidity. Striped ginger (*Alpinia zerumbet variegata*) and peacock gingers (*Kaempferia* spp.) are mostly grown for their leaves, but hedychiums are worthwhile for their fragrant flowers atop narrow stalks and are natural additions to a planting with other fragrant plants. Chinese evergreen is the common name for plants in the *Aglaonema* genus, but most of the cultivars you'll see are so much more than just green. The dark green foliage is usually painted with layers of silver, red, and sage. Dumb cane (*Dieffenbachia*) is an old standby that often goes unnoticed when planted in hospitals and shopping malls, but their bright and variegated leaves really stand out in the center of darker plants in an arrangement.

They might not be as impressive as the other plants in this section, but peace lilies (*Spathiphyllum*) are reliable and graceful additions to any arrangement. They're also very easy to find at larger retailers at any time of the year. Most grow them for the white sails formed by the white spathes covering their flowers, but their long deep green leaves manage to look lush and classy even when out of bloom. Cast iron plants (*Aspidistra*) are appropriately named for their durable and strappy emerald green leaves that stay attractive even through neglect in the darkest parts of the home.

PROLIFIC BLOOMERS

Houseplants are usually grown for their colorful foliage rather than their flowers, because the heaviest bloomers typically require more sunlight and maintenance than most can provide. Still, the possibility of cheery flowers on a cold winter morning is just too good to pass up, and flowers bring a sense of being in a real garden to indoor plantings.

Lantanas (*L. camara* and *L. montevidensis*) are rangy woody plants that bloom almost year-round with inch-wide clusters of flowers ranging from red to yellow and from lavender to white. Trailing varieties are the best for container plantings. Pentas (*Pentas lanceolata*) also provide colorful flowers on small plants but bloom in colors like crimson and pink. Choose smaller dwarf varieties if you'll be using them at the edge of a planting.

Upright bloomers like the shrimp plant (*Justicia brandegeana*) and the lollipop plant (*Pachystachys lutea*) can serve as focal points along with foliage plants or be grouped together with other fine-textured bloomers for a naturalistic planting. Small-leaved blooming shrubs such as the bottlebrush (*Callistemon viminalis*

Callistemon viminalis *'Little John' is a very prolific bloomer.*

'Little John') and powderpuff plant (*Calliandra haematocephala* 'Nana') can have their lower limbs removed to look more like trees (called "standards") and make room for more plants.

When only a temporary burst of flower power is needed, add short-lived seasonal houseplants like mums (*Chrysanthemum morifolium*) and cyclamens (*Cyclamen persicum*) to container combos and replace them with another plant when they start to decline.

Haworthia species are more tolerant of low light than most other succulents.

SUCCULENTS FOR LOW LIGHT

Out of the succulents that can handle low light, snake plants (*Sansevieria*) rule the roost. The slow-growing plants tolerate lower light than any other succulent and have been gracing the darkest rooms of our homes for decades. The most common one is *Sansevieria trifasciata laurentii*, but don't stop there! 'Bantel's Sensation' has narrower leaves that are heavily striped with white, 'Moonshine' has leaves that are a silvery sage green, and *Sansevieria cylindrica* is notable for bearing tubular leaves instead of the usual flattened ones. Bird's nest snake plants such as 'Hahnii' are shorter and useful as a low-growing filler in arrangements.

Haworthias and gasterias are low-growing succulents from South Africa that provide the same look of a typical succulent planting while tolerating less light. Haworthias are a mixed bag of about 140 different species ranging from the clear and glassy leaves of the window plant (*H. cooperi*) to the narrow white-striped dark green leaves of the zebra plant (*H. attenuata*). Gasterias are usually distinguished by their tendency to overlap leaves atop each other when young, rather than in the familiar spirals seen in haworthias and other succulents. A common one to look for is ox tongue (*Gasteria bicolor*). Though these plants tolerate indirect light, they positively thrive with a little direct sunshine from an east- or west-facing window.

SUCCULENTS FOR SUN

Where to begin? If you have an unobstructed window facing in any direction other than north, you can partake in the myriad shapes and colors of the sun-loving succulents. Among the smaller succulents, echeverias are some of the most common, and their pastel rosettes look very much like powdery roses. Stonecrops range from the miniscule leaves of the goldmoss stonecrop (*Sedum acre*) to monsters like burro's tail (*Sedum morganianum*) and jelly bean plant (*Sedum rubrotinctum*). Ghost plants (*Graptopetalum*) look like a cross between an echeveria and a sedum, and are even hybridized with them to create plants that show off the best of both worlds! Crassulas are quite diverse and run the gamut from the ubiquitous jade plant to the mind-blowing, nearly perfectly symmetrical stacked leaves of *Crassula perforata* and 'Buddha's Temple'. Most of the crassulas are excellent additions to an undersea-themed planting design.

If those all seemed like a bunch of softies, step into the ring with these vicious man-eaters. The small tiger's jaws plant (*Faucaria*) is especially interesting for its harmless toothy leaf margins, and the much larger *Dyckia* 'Cherry Coke' has fierce spines on stiff, deep burgundy leaves. The spiky tipped agaves are always down for a good fight, but it's best to use smaller ones like *A. victoriae-reginae* or *A. parviflora* in the cramped confines of a home. There are far more choices when it comes to their counterparts from across the Atlantic, the aloes. You can grow *Aloe vera* indoors, but its sloppy form and uninteresting leaves pale in comparison to others in your arsenal. Spotted aloe (*Aloe maculata*) makes for a nice centerpiece when surrounded by other succulents, as does tree aloe (*Aloe arborescens*). For smaller and more versatile plants in the genus, look no further than such gems as lacy aloe (*Aloe aristata*) and the tiny Aloe *humilis*.

Agave parryi *prefers lots of sunlight.*

Episcia makes a fine trailing companion for the upright rattlesnake plant.

VINES AND TRAILERS

Not all vines are cut out for mixed plantings, and many of them are just too rambunctious to behave alongside other plants. The exotic-looking passionflower (*Passiflora*) and lushly growing grape ivy are both wonderful plants but would need frequent pruning and a support such as a trellis or stakes. If you can provide a little humidity, look for trailing vines like the free flowering lipstick plant (*Aeschynanthus lobbianus*), chocolate soldier (*Episcia*), and goldfish plant (*Columnea banksii*).

Wax vines (*Hoya carnosa*) were popular as houseplants for their durability and fragrant waxy blooms long ago but have only recently made a comeback. Along with the other *Hoya* species and the related *Dischidia* plants, these epiphytic milkweed (yes, milkweed!) plants are just now becoming popular in hanging baskets at large retailers and rightly so. They can survive weeks without water and, if planted in free-draining orchid mix or bark, can be watered as often as you'd like. The best mixture consists of two parts orchid mix and one part regular mix. If adding them to non-epiphytic plantings, amend the surrounding soil with orchid mix so that the roots can breathe. *Dischidia* plants are even more epiphytic and are best planted in orchid mix, bark, or sphagnum moss. Keep the medium lightly moist to the touch, allowing it to dry out between waterings.

If humidity is a problem, there are lots of easy trailing plants from which you can choose. Strawberry begonia (*Saxifraga*), mistletoe cactus (*Rhipsalis*), and even spider plant (*Chlorophytum*) are all easy to care for. The drought-tolerant trailers in the spiderwort family make excellent trailing plants for sunny plantings and are easily grown from cuttings. Wandering Jew (*Tradescantia zebrina*) has long been a favorite for hanging baskets, and its metallic leaves of purple, silver, and sage work well in groupings where a bit of color is needed. The pointed leaves of purple heart (*T. pallida*) are an even more intense hue of purple, but they're also coarser and a bit less tidy. There are even spiderworts (*T. sillamontana* and *Cyanotis somaliensis*) with soft and woolly sage leaves that are soft to the touch.

PLANT LISTS

Because I want *you* to design your own exciting combinations of compatible plants, I've put together some helpful lists to help you pick the right ones. The lists are grouped by some common element. Please note these Latin names are generally italicized in garden books, but for ease of reading, I've left most of them in Roman type.

BY USES

TEMPORARY HOUSEPLANTS

If you've managed to kill one of these short-lived seasonal houseplants, don't beat yourself up about it. Even though they don't last very long, that doesn't mean you can't use them in your arrangements for seasonal displays. When the last bloom (or leaf) drops, remove the plant entirely and replace it with another plant and fresh potting mix.

- Achimenes
- Begonia (some)
- Browallia
- Celosia
- Cineraria
- Chrysanthemum
- Coleus
- Crocus
- Cyclamen
- Dahlia
- Dianthus
- Euphorbia (some)
- Exacum
- Freesia
- Fuchsia
- Gardenia
- Gerbera
- Hibiscus
- Hyacinthus
- Impatiens
- Iris
- Jasminum
- Lilium
- Muscari
- Narcissus
- Poinsettia
- Primula
- Rosa
- Senecio
- Sinningia
- Tulipa

Poinsettia

EDIBLE HOUSEPLANTS

Does it get any better than growing exotic fruit in the comfort of your own home? From herbs like mint (*Mentha*) and lemongrass (*Cymbopogon*) to exotic fruit trees like starfruit (*Carambola*) and pineapple guava (*Feijoa*), these tasty indoor plants will add flavor to your container gardens.

Starfruit

- Ananas
- Capsicum
- Carambola
- Citrus
- Eriobotrya
- Eugenia
- Feijoa
- Ficus carica
- Fortunella
- Glycosmis
- Hylocereus
- Mentha
- Plectranthus (some)
- Psidium
- Punica
- Rosmarinus
- Thymus
- Zingiber zerumbet

TRAILING AND VINING HOUSEPLANTS

Place these houseplants at the edge of your arrangements so that they can tumble down over the lip of the pot for a natural look. They're especially useful for small spaces and can be trimmed occasionally as needed. Train them up a trellis at the rear of plantings for even more impact.

- Aeschynanthus
- Allamanda
- Ceropegia
- Chlorophytum
- Cissus
- Columnea
- Episcia
- Ficus pumila
- Gloriosa
- Gynura
- Hatiora
- Hedera
- Hoya
- Lantana
- Mikania
- Peperomia (some)
- Philodendron
- Pilea (some)
- Rhipsalis
- Russelia
- Saxifraga
- Scindapsus
- Sedum
- Selaginella
- Senecio
- Setcreasea
- Stapelia
- Tradescantia

Episcia

Schefflera

STRUCTURAL HOUSEPLANTS

These bold and dramatic plants with large leaves often make up the "thrillers" in an arrangement. They are best situated in the center or rear of container arrangements so that they don't cover up the shorter houseplants in the grouping.

- Aechmea
- Agave
- Aglaonema
- Araucaria
- Aspidistra
- Calathea
- Chamaedorea
- Clivia
- Cordyline
- Crinum
- Dieffenbachia
- Dracaena
- Euphorbia (some)
- Fatshedera

- Ficus (some)
- Heliconia
- Howea
- Monstera
- Pandanus
- Philodendron (birds nest types)
- Rhapis
- Sansevieria
- Schefflera
- Strelitzia
- Vriesea
- Yucca

BUSHY HOUSEPLANTS

Bushy houseplants are useful in container combos for their versatility. Use the smallest of these to fill out the space between other plants, and allow the larger ones to become the focal points. Many can be pruned to shape thanks to their branching habit.

- Acalypha
- Achimenes
- Aucuba
- Begonia
- Breynia
- Calliandra
- Callistemon

- Capsicum
- Chrysanthemum
- Citrus
- Cleyera
- Coffea
- Coleus
- Crassula

Acalypha

- Euonymus
- Ficus (some)
- Fittonia
- Gardenia
- Hatiora
- Lantana
- Laurus
- Leea
- Nerium (dwarf)
- Osmanthus
- Pachystachys
- Pelargonium
- Pentas
- Peperomia (some)
- Pilea (some)
- Pittosporum
- Plectranthus
- Plumbago
- Podocarpus
- Pseuderanthemum
- Radermachera
- Rhododendron
- Schefflera
- Strobilanthes

PLANTS FOR MINIATURE COMBINATIONS

Use these low-growing plants as groundcovers in your container combinations or use them in miniature gardens so they resemble tiny garden plants. Some such as mondo grass (*Ophiopogon*) last for a long time while others like polka dot plant (*Hypoestes*) should be replaced as they start to decline.

- Acorus
- Aloe (some)
- Carex
- Crassula
- Cryptanthus
- Davallia
- Faucaria
- Ficus (some)
- Fittonia
- Gasteria
- Haworthia
- Hypoestes
- Impatiens
- Nertera
- Ophiopogon
- Mammillaria
- Pellaea
- Peperomia (some)
- Pilea (some)
- Rhipsalis
- Sagina
- Sansevieria (some)
- Saxifraga
- Sedum
- Selaginella
- Senecio (succulents)
- Solanum
- Tillandsia
- Zephyanthes

Selaginella

HOUSEPLANTS WITH UNUSUAL TEXTURES

- Asparagus plumosus
- Ceropegia woodii
- Cissus discolor
- Cotyledon ladismithiensis
- Cyanotis somaliensis
- Gynura aurantiaca
- Huernia scheideriana
- Kalanchoe tomentosa
- Microsorum musifolium
- Pilea 'Moon Valley'
- Stapelia gigantea
- Tradescantia sillamontana

WHITE OR GREEN

- Aspidistra elatior variegata
- Chlorophytum comosum vittatum
- Dieffenbachia 'Tropic Snow'
- Dracaena fragrans 'White Stripe'
- Epipremnum aureus 'Marble Queen'
- Ficus benjamina 'Starlight'
- Ficus elastica 'Tricolor'
- Ficus pumila var. 'Variegata'
- Peperomia caperata variegata
- Peperomia magnoliaefolia variegata
- Plectranthus amboinicus 'Variegatus'
- Monstera deliciosa variegata
- Neoregelia carolinae tricolor
- Saxifraga sarmentosa tricolor
- Tradescantia fluminensis 'Quicksilver'
- Tradescantia spathacea

DEEP BLUE-GREEN

- Aglaonema commutatum
- Alocasia x amazonica
- Aloe variegata
- Anthurium crystallinum
- Aphelandra squarrosa
- Calathea insignis
- Cereus peruvianus monstrose
- Cissus discolor
- Columnea banksii
- Cyanotis somaliensis
- Dieffenbachia amoena
- Dracaena fragrans 'Janet Craig Compacta'
- Ficus benjamina 'Midnight'
- Ficus elastica 'Decora'
- Gasteria bicolor
- Haworthia margaritifera
- Podocarpus macrophyllus
- Sansevieria 'Hahnii'
- Sansevieria trifasciata
- Schefflera elegantissima
- Selaginella uncinata
- Vreisea hieroglyphica
- Vriesea splendens

LIME OR CHARTRUESE

- Acorus gramineus 'Ogon'
- Alternanthera 'Solid Yellow'
- Asplenium nidus
- Begonia 'Leopon'
- Cordyline terminalis 'Kiwi'
- Dracaena fragrans 'Limelight'
- Dracaena fragrans lindenii
- Dracaena fragrans 'Massangeana'
- Dracaena reflexa
- Epipremnum aureum 'Neon'
- Ficus benjamina 'Margarita'
- Iresine herbstii aureoreticulata
- Neoregelia cruenta
- Nephrolepis 'Tiger Fern'
- Pedilanthus tithymaloides
- Pelargonium crispum
- Pilea 'Moon Valley'
- Philodendron hederaceum 'Lemon Lime'
- Selaginella kraussiana 'Aurea'
- Solenostemon 'Chartreuse'

SAGE OR SILVER

- Aechmea fasciata
- Aglaonema 'Silver Queen'
- Callisia gentlei var. elegans
- Callistemon citrinus 'Little John'
- Cephalocereus senilis
- Cyanotis somaliensis
- Dyckia marnier-lapostollei
- Echeveria elegans
- Episcia 'Silver Sheen'
- Episcia 'Spearmint'
- Ficus benjamina 'Variegata'
- Ficus elastica 'Schrijveriana'
- Fortunella 'Centennial'
- Graptopetalum paraguayense
- Hedera helix 'Eva'
- Kalanchoe tomentosa
- Maranta leuconeura kerchoveana
- Peperomia argyreia
- Peperomia scandens variegata
- Pilea glauca
- Pilea pubescens 'Silver Cloud'

Graptopetalum

- Pittosporum tobira variegata
- Scindapsus pictus 'Argyaeus'
- Sedum morganianum
- Tillandsia ionatha
- Tillandsia xerographica
- Tradescantia sillamontana
- Tradescantia spathacea

NEARLY BLACK

- Aeonium arboretum 'Zwartkop'
- Begonia 'Mo Reese'
- Begonia 'Texastar'
- Begonia 'Withlacoochee'
- Cordyline 'Black Magic'
- Cryptanthus 'Black Mystic'
- Cryptanthus zonatus
- Dyckia 'Black Gold'
- Episcia 'Chocolate Velour'
- Ficus elastica 'Black Prince'
- Fittonia albivenis Argyroneura group
- Hemigraphis alternata 'Exotica'
- Maranta leuconeura massangeana
- Nematanthus 'Tropicana'
- Neoregelia 'Pitch Black'
- Ophiopogon planiscapus 'Nigrescens'
- Orthophytum gurkenii
- Peperomia caperata 'Metallic Gray'
- Philodendron melanochrysum
- Pilea involucrata 'Norfolk'
- Schefflera elegantissima

PURPLE OR BRONZE

- Aechmea 'Burgundy'
- Aechmea 'Foster's Favorite'
- Aeonium arboreum 'Atropurpureum'
- Billbergia amoena 'Red'
- Crinum augustum
- Gynura aurantiaca
- Gymnocalycium mihanovichii var. friedrichiiIresine herbstii
- Neoregelia 'Fireball'
- Neoregelia 'Tangerine'
- Philodendron 'Burgundy'
- Strobilanthes dyeranus
- Tradescantia pallida
- Tradescantia zebrina
- Vriesea sucrei

PINK

- Aglaonema 'Siam Aurora'
- Ananas comosus 'Variegatus'
- Begonia rex 'Pink'
- Breynia disticha 'Roseo-picta'
- Calathea ornata
- Cryptanthus 'Pink Blush'
- Dracaena marginata 'Colorama'
- Echeveria agavoides 'Lipstick'
- Episcia 'Strawberry Patch'
- Ficus elastica 'Ruby'
- Ficus elastica 'Tricolor'
- Hypoestes phyllostachya
- Neoregelia 'Sexy Pink'
- Oxalis 'Plum Crazy'
- Peperomia caperata 'Schumi Red'
- Syngonium 'Regina Red'

Neoregelia

GOLD OR ORANGE

- Acalypha wilkesiana
- Aucuba japonica
- Begonia 'Vivaldi'
- Chlorophytum 'Fireflash'
- Codiaeum variegatum 'Petra'
- Dracaena surculosa 'Florida Beauty'
- Epipremnum aureus 'Golden Queen'
- Neoregelia 'Aztec'
- Oxalis spiralis subsp. vulcanicola 'Sunset Velvet'
- Pereskia aculeata 'Godselffiana' variegata
- Philodendron 'Prince of Orange'
- Sansevieria 'Golden Hahnii'
- Sansevieria trifasciata laurentii
- Sedum rubrotinctum
- Solenostemon 'Rustic Orange

BY NEEDS

EASY PLANTS

These plants are not only incredibly easy to grow, but they are diverse and colorful enough to make your container plantings stand out. Many included here are especially rewarding because they're easily multiplied by cuttings or offsets.

- Aglaonema
- Asplenium (birds nest types)
- Beaucarnea
- Chamaedorea
- Cryptanthus
- Dieffenbachia
- Dracaena
- Epiphyllum
- Epipremnum
- Haworthia
- Hoya
- Peperomia (most)
- Philodendron
- Rhipsalis
- Sansevieria
- Saxifraga
- Scindapsus
- Yucca

MORE DIFFICULT PLANTS

These are seductive and exciting plants for the most adventurous interior gardeners. Some, such as hibiscus and gardenias, need lots of air movement and humidity and are practically pest magnets even if those conditions are met. Living stones (*Lithops* and *Conophytum*) have very specific dormancy periods and have been known to disappear overnight if they're watered in summer or winter.

- Alocasia
- Begonia (rex)
- Camellia
- Codiaeum
- Conophytum
- Gardenia
- Heliconia
- Hibiscus
- Ixora
- Lithops
- Medinilla
- Selaginella

PLANTS TO WATER LESS IN WINTER

Most houseplants can be watered less in winter, but these plants may actually decline if the soil stays too moist. A lot of these are succulents originally from climates with winter dry seasons, so plant them with durable drought-tolerant plants such as those listed in "Easy Plants" or "Sunny and Dry."

- Adenium
- Aloe (some)
- Ceropegia
- Cissus
- Dorstenia
- Echeveria
- Euphorbia (succulent types)
- Huernia
- Jatropha
- Lithops
- Pachypodium
- Pedilanthus
- Plumeria
- Tillandsia

Hatiora

PLANTS THAT NEED COOL WINTERS

- Aucuba
- Azalea
- Camellia
- Clivia
- Euonymus
- Fuschia
- Hatiora
- Hydrangea
- Pittosporum
- Plumbago
- Podocarpus

PLANTS THAT NEED HUMIDITY

- Adiantum
- Alpinia
- Ananus
- Anthurium
- Breynia
- Caladium
- Calliandra
- Cattleya
- Chamaedorea
- Coleus
- Columnea
- Cordyline fruticosa
- Costus
- Davallia
- Dischidia
- Episcia
- Fittonia
- Gardenia
- Hedera
- Hedychium
- Heliconia
- Hemigraphis
- Hoya (some)
- Hypoestes
- Ixora
- Lycopodium
- Maranta
- Medinilla
- Musa
- Nematanthus
- Nephrolepis
- Pandanus
- Peperomia (some)
- Philodendron (some)
- Pilea
- Platycerium
- Plumeria
- Pseuderanthemum
- Pteris
- Sanchezia
- Saintpaulia
- Selaginella
- Strobilanthes
- Tillandsia
- Vanda

Callliandra

EPIPHYTES

Epiphytes are a very special group of plants that can survive on the bark of trees without any soil. For the indoor gardener, this means that they can be planted on a wide variety of surfaces, including driftwood, grapevine wreaths, in orchid bark—or in the case of Tillandsias, hanging from nothing more than a string. The creative possibilities are endless!

There are a lot of epiphytes used in this book, and for good reason. They're flexible and fun! Most of the bromeliads and epiphytic cacti (*Rhipsalis, Hatiora*, and so forth) can just be plugged into almost any container combination, with or without root space. Most are drought tolerant, but a few need humidity.

Epiphyte

- Aechmea
- Asplenium (birds nest types)
- Billbergia
- Encyclia
- Epidendrum
- Epiphyllum
- Guzmania
- Hatiora
- Hoya
- Neoregelia
- Nidularium
- Oncidium
- Phalaenopsis
- Phlebodium
- Pseudorhipsalis
- Rhipsalis
- Schlumbergera
- Tillandsia
- Vanda
- Vriesea

PLANTS FOR LOW LIGHT

Not many plants will thrive in a dimly lit room, but the ones listed here do it better than the rest. Plants grown in low light grow more slowly and require less water, but ferns and spikemosses will still need constant moisture and humidity.

- Aglaonema
- Aspidistra
- Asplenium
- Chamaedorea
- Davallia
- Epipremnum
- Peperomia
- Philodendron
- Sansevieria
- Selaginella
- Zamioculcas

BRIGHT AND DRY

Though many plants will tolerate drought and a lack of direct light, these survivors will actually perform well under these conditions.

- Aloe (some)
- Aspidistra
- Beaucarnea
- Bromeliad
- Crassula (some)
- Cycas
- Dischidia
- Epiphyllum
- Euphorbia
- Gasteria
- Haworthia
- Hoya
- Huernia
- Pedilanthus
- Peperomia
- Rhipsalis
- Sansevieria
- Stapelia
- Yucca

BRIGHT AND MOIST

Most houseplants fall under this category: Bright and indirect light planted in potting mix that doesn't dry out for too long. Some of these plants will tolerate drought longer than others.

- Acorus
- Aeschynanthus
- Agapanthus
- Aglaonema
- Alocasia
- Alpinia
- Ananus
- Anthurium
- Aphelandra
- Araucaria
- Ardisia
- Asparagus
- Aspidistra
- Asplenium
- Aucuba
- Begonia
- Beaucarnea
- Blechnum
- Bulbine
- Caladium
- Calathea
- Camellia
- Carissa
- Caryota
- Cattleya
- Chirita
- Chlorophytum
- Cissus
- Citrus
- Clerodendrum
- Coffea
- Coccoloba
- Cordyline
- Costus
- Crinum
- Crossandra
- Ctenanthe
- Cuphea

Cyclamen

- Curcuma
- Cycas
- Cyclamen
- Cymbidium

- Cyperus
- Cyrtomium
- Davallia
- Dypsis
- Echeveria
- Epiphyllum
- Epipremnum
- Eucomis
- Fatshedera
- Fatsia
- Ficus
- Fuchsia
- Guzmania
- Gynura
- Hedychium
- Heliconia
- Hemigraphis
- Hippeastrum
- Homalomena
- Howea
- Impatiens
- Jacobinia
- Justicia
- Leea
- Lilium
- Liriope
- Ludisia
- Maranta
- Medinilla
- Mikania
- Mimosa
- Monstera
- Nandina
- Nephrolepis
- Nertera
- Ophiopogon
- Oxalis
- Pachira
- Paphiopedilum
- Pelargonium
- Pentas
- Peperomia
- Phalaenopsis
- Philodendron
- Pilea
- Pittosporum
- Plectranthus
- Plumbago
- Plumeria
- Podocarpus
- Pogonatherum
- Poinsettia
- Polyscias
- Pseuderanthemum
- Radermachera
- Rhipsalis
- Rhododendron
- Rhoeo
- Ruellia
- Saintpaulia
- Sanchezia
- Saxifraga
- Scadoxus
- Schefflera
- Scindapsus
- Soleirolia
- Solenostemon
- Spathiphyllum
- Strelitzia
- Streptocarpus
- Strobilanthes
- Stromanthe
- Syngonium
- Tolmiea
- Vriesea
- Yucca
- Zamioculcas
- Zantedeschia

SUNNY AND DRY

This is the domain of cacti, succulents, and other desert dwellers. Cactus potting mix is ideal, and it should dry out between waterings. Some prefer drier conditions in winter, others in summer; these are also noted in a list on page 60.

- Adenium
- Aeonium
- Agave
- Aloe
- Aporocactus
- Beaucarnea
- Bulbine
- Cereus
- Ceropegia
- Cotyledon
- Crassula
- Dyckia

Dyckia

- Echeveria
- Echinocactus
- Echinopsis
- Euphorbia
- Ferocactus
- Faucaria
- Gasteria
- Graptopetalum
- Gymnocalycium
- Haworthia
- Jatropha
- Kalanchoe (some)
- Lithops

- Mammillaria
- Opuntia
- Pachypodium
- Peperomia (window leaf)
- Pereskia
- Portulaca

- Portulacaria
- Rebutia
- Sedum
- Senecio
- Yucca

SUNNY AND MOIST

Most plants in this category are grown for their flowers. Many choices from the "Bright and Moist" category will also do well if planted in the shade of these plants in a west- or east-facing window but only if you slowly transition them to the brighter light.

Oxalis

- Abutilon
- Acalypha
- Agapanthus
- Allamanda
- Ananus
- Bougainvillea
- Bulbine
- Callistemon
- Carissa
- Coccoloba
- Curcuma
- Dyckia
- Epidendrum (reed stems)
- Euphorbia milii
- Iresine
- Ixora

- Jasminum
- Kalanchoe
- Lantana
- Mimosa
- Nandina
- Nerium (water sparingly in winter)
- Oxalis
- Punica
- Serissa
- Solenostemon
- Strelitzia
- Strobilanthes
- Tradescantia (less in winter)
- Yucca (less in winter)

HOW TO USE THIS BOOK

I've used a "cookbook" approach to these container combinations by creating plant "recipes," each with a list of ingredients and how to create it. Each recipe will have a different level of light, moisture, and humidity. I also share any special planting tips, and important watering, fertilizing, or pest-control tips.

WHAT'S THE SHOPPING LIST?

The shopping list tells you the ingredients you'll need for your recipe, including the type of potting mix, the size of container, extra decorative touches, amendments, and, of course, the plants. First, I list the number of plants you'll need, their common name, and then their Latin name, complete with the specific cultivar, hybrid, or variety that I happened to use. The "plant-a-gram" letter refers to the planting diagram showing how I positioned the plants.

WHAT IF I CAN'T FIND THE PLANTS?

No problem! If you can't find the plants at a garden center or online nursery, just refer to the Plant Options with each recipe, where I list other plants that I recommend. There is also a detailed list of plants starting on page 53 so that you can make your own matches. Don't be afraid to deviate from the recipe!

WHAT SIZE PLANTS DO I NEED?

Container sizes for houseplants are really a mixed bag, and unlike outdoor bedding flowers, there's no telling what size pot your plant will occupy. Whenever possible, opt for smaller plants. They're more affordable, offer the most versatility, and will eventually fill in to cover the gaps. Most important, you can fit more of them in a pot. Adjust the recipes as needed so that you can fit the plants into your container; it needs to feel complete.

Choose the plants for your container garden to complement one another.

THE RECIPES

Are you ready to get started? Then use this "cookbook" of ideas and inspiration to create your own artistic indoor garden creations. If you're the kind of person who would rather buy the outfit on the mannequin in the window, then follow the recipes to a tee and hunt down each of the plants at your garden center or online (page 170) to recreate what I've done. If you're the kind of person who'd rather make your own outfit, look at these as examples to get you started on your own creative interpretations. Just make sure you still read the descriptions, though, because they have a lot of helpful information. Here are some of the things I've taken into account.

How They'll Grow: I've planted each of these recipes myself, so I give specific advice pertaining to each combo and its plants. I've even tested many of these combinations myself by growing them in my home over the course of several months, so I can also tell you how they'll grow together. In many cases the combos will look even better with time, but I'll also tell you which combos will need sprucing up down the road.

What Sizes to Use: The plants you would use for outdoor container combinations usually come in small pots, but because houseplants come in all sizes, I've designed these recipes to be flexible for you to work with what's available. If you have a houseplant that's too large for the space in the combo, try separating it by taking divisions or cuttings. To get the look of a larger houseplant, combine two to three smaller houseplants together.

How to Get Your Plants: Another way houseplants differ from outdoor plants is that there is usually a much smaller selection available at the garden center. To make this easier for you, I've provided replacements for each recipe, included a list of compatible plants, and provided links of online nurseries. If you bring this book to your local garden center and show them the plant you need, they're usually more than willing to order one for you—but if they don't have a supplier, I've listed a few wholesale nurseries.

Where to Grow Them: Each recipe is different, and some have to be treated with special care. Every entry has unique instructions regarding light, humidity, temperature, and other requirements. Not only do I tell you where they'll do best, I also tell you where they'll *look* best, and how to make them stand out in your own uniquely decorated home.

Back in Style

LIGHT	MOISTURE	HUMIDITY
Low to bright	Average to moist	Average to high

Shopping List

- Large container
- Regular potting mix
- Coir
- **A** 1 peace lily *(Spathiphyllum wallisii)*
- **B** 1 peacock plant *(Calathea makoyana)*
- **C** 1 marble pothos
  (Epipremnum aureum 'Marble Queen')

Plant Options

Swap out the peacock plant with one of its relatives if you can't find it at the garden center. Calathea ornata, Maranta tricolor, *and* Maranta leuconeura *have similar patterning and are all great choices. The peace lily can be replaced with a Chinese evergreen, and satin pothos is a great substitute for the marble pothos.*

Houseplants have been in and out of style a lot by now, but some plants still bring to mind outmoded trends like macramé and Hawaiian kitsch. So how do you jazz up plants as passé and boring as peace lilies and pothos? By putting them in a fancy pot and adding a little something special to make them pop, of course! *Calathea makoyana* is a spectacular relative of the prayer plant with striking striped leaves of deep green and sage, and the markings resonate well with the ceramic urn's pattern and the shape of the peace lily's leaves. The energetic lines keep your eyes moving around the whole composition, yet the subdued color scheme feels restful and refined. The peace lily and pothos certainly contribute to the design as well, yet neither stands out nor calls too much attention to itself. Despite the graceful white sails that surround the peace lily's blooms, there is no showboating. Each plant works in tandem to make an elegant display that never goes out of style.

Like most *Calathea* plants, the peacock plant loves moist soil and humidity. Add coir to the potting mix to help it last longer between waterings, and provide humidity by placing the container in a well-lit bathroom or by misting occasionally. Remove spent flowers from the peace lily and peacock plant as they turn brown, and prune the pothos if it begins to get out of control.

Blissfully Balinese

LIGHT	MOISTURE	HUMIDITY
Bright to sunny	Average	Average to high

Shopping List

- Extra-large container
- **(A)** 1 ti plant (*Cordyline fruticosa* cv.)
- **(B)** 2 macho ferns
  (*Nephrolepsis biserrata*)
- **(C)** 3 oyster plants (*Rhoeodiscolor*)
- **(D)** 1 bromeliad (*Neoregelia* hybrid)

Plant Options

Since the macho fern can get quite large, find a smaller replacement for your limited space. Almost any fern will work, but rabbit foot ferns (Davallia spp.) and maidenhair ferns (Adiantum spp.) get my pick for their delicate foliage and would look great with waffle plants replacing the oyster plants.

I've always been enamored with the gardens of the Balinese landscape architect Made Wijaya, and thought it would be fun to borrow a little bit of tropical inspiration for a container garden. It might not win any awards for authenticity but still manages to remind me of a photo I once saw of Wijaya's Bali Hyatt gardens, covered by huge swaths of colorful groundcovers with enthusiastic bursts of ti plants and agave scattered throughout. I've included ti plants and oyster plants in my version but have also added ferns to impart that quintessential Balinese rainforest lushness. But first, a word of warning: The macho fern planted in the rear can get very, very big if given enough time to take over in true macho fashion. To see just how massive they can get, turn to page 23 or look at the planter in the backdrop of this photo to see a glimpse into the future. It's the very same fern with the very same ti plant, photographed many years after being planted and swallowing up the entire area with its lovely apple green foliage. To tie in with the macho ferns, maidenhair fern was planted in between the oyster plants where they spill over the pot's edge.

If there's one thing that these plants require, it's humidity. With a container this large, humidity is best provided by placing it in a conservatory, sunroom, or well-lit bathroom. Otherwise plan on dealing with brown and crispy leaf tips until spring, when the whole planting can be brought outdoors to a shady area. Spider mites are sometimes a problem on ti plants grown in dry air. Prevent and remove them by running a damp rag over each leaf whenever dust begins to accumulate. Remove lower leaves as they turn brown, as the leaf axils sometimes harbor pests. If the ferns become unmanageably large, shear them down to a couple of inches above their crowns and divide them with a sharp knife, replacing soil after removal.

A Brimming Urn

LIGHT	MOISTURE	HUMIDITY
Bright	Average to high	Average to high

Shopping List

- Medium container
- Regular potting mix
- **(A)** 2 firecracker plants
  (*Russelia equisetiformis*)
- **(B)** 2 table ferns
  (*Pteris ensiformis victoriae*)

Plant Options

*These two plants look beautiful together, but they both have different lighting preferences. For sunnier situations, replace the table fern with a cigar plant (*Cuphea*) or a shrimp plant (*Justicia brandegeana*). For shadier spots, replace the firecracker plant with a draping fern such as* Nephrolepis *'Fluffy Ruffles' or* Selaginella uncinata.

If A Brimming Urn combo isn't even better than having a brimming water feature in your home, it's almost certainly the *next* best thing. Silvery table ferns appear to splash out of the sides, while feathery firecracker plants rush over the edge with little exclamation points of tubular red flowers. The firecracker plant's colorful stems provide plenty of interest on their own, and it's not unusual to find colors ranging from dark green to chartreuse or pink, all on the same plant. Unlike many of the container combos in this book, there is no clear focal point other than the arrangement itself, which gives the whole composition a sense of calm and serenity despite the energetic plants within. Take the pot outside in summer to enjoy the sight of hummingbirds flitting about and drinking from the blooms, or just use it to create a feeling of calm in your outdoor living area. I prefer the clean, calming appearance of these two plants, but if you need a little more pizzazz, turn the fountain into fireworks by adding a dracaena as a dynamic centerpiece.

Give these feathery plants bright indirect light and consistent moisture. The fern requires humidity but can be swapped out in drier environments. The firecracker plant will eventually put out longer stems that might even reach the ground. You can either cut the longest ones back to the base, move the plants to a larger container, or just enjoy the overgrown pot as it cascades over the floor in a shower of fireworks. As with most blooming houseplants, be prepared to pick up the firecracker plant's flower petals as they fall. Place the planter on a solid surface of tile, wood, or stone to let the petals collect to form a carpet of brilliant red blooms. To keep the firecracker plant blooming years after planting, fertilize with a product high in potassium.

Burgundy Bliss

LIGHT	MOISTURE	HUMIDITY
Bright to sunny	Low to average	Average

Shopping List

- Large container
- Cactus potting mix
- (A) 3 fireball bromeliads
  (*Neoregelia* 'Fireball')
- (B) 1 striped matchstick bromeliad
  (*Aechmea cylindrata*)
- (C) 3 creeping sedums
  (*Sedum lineare* 'Sea Urchin')

Plant Options

Other bromeliads can replace the fireball bromeliads, but try to find some with small rosettes and a stoloniferous (branching) habit. 'Zoe' is similar but has light stripes down the center of each leaf. Sedums can be replaced with another succulent with silver or sage leaves, and the architectural look of the striped matchstick bromeliad can be attained with a larger succulent such as an agave *or* aloe.

If you have to choose one bromeliad for your container combinations, I urge you to give *Neoregelia* 'Fireball' a shot. The fireball bromeliad is a bit of a shapeshifter, keeping its tight burgundy rosettes when grown in a sunny windowsill, or reverting to arching glossy green leaves if grown in lower light. Not only do the color and form change to suit that environment, it also handles anything from moist soil to no soil at all and can be grown along with all but the thirstiest houseplants. To best show off the dramatic color they take on when grown in the sun, I've used it as a backdrop behind another bromeliad, the white-striped *Aechmea cylindrata*. If the variegated leaves weren't cool enough, stick around until it produces its tall matchstick blooms of pink and blue on a tall stem! A groundcover of *Sedum* 'Sea Urchin' echoes the color and pattern of the striped bromeliad, while the wide oxblood bowl holding it all together ties in nicely with the fireball bromeliads as well as traditional styles of interior décor.

Maintenance is blissfully easy with this grouping of epiphytes and succulents, but you might want to place the combo on a floor or surface that you don't mind getting a little wet. This is because each of the overhanging fireball bromeliads will need water in each of the cups, but it's a lot easier if you use a mister. Train the bromeliads to grow upward with the assistance of stakes or a trellis, or just allow them to grow freely over the side. Either way, they'll produce tiny purple blooms in the vases before forming new offsets. Root offsets and cuttings of each plant as desired, according to the instructions on page 37. Fertilizer will actually make the colors of the bromeliads less intense, but if they start to lose their vigor, feed with a quick pick-me-up of diluted orchid fertilizer at half the recommended amount or use compost tea.

Café Au Lait

LIGHT	MOISTURE	HUMIDITY
Sunny	Average	Low

Shopping List

- Extra-small container
- Cactus mix
- **(A)** 1 queen's tears (*Billbergia hoelscheriana*)
- **(B)** 1 partridge breast aloe
  (*Aloe variegata* 'Gator')
- **(C)** 1 echeveria (*Echeveria* 'Lola')
- **(D)** 1 sea urchin stonecrop
  (*Sedum* 'Sea Urchin')

Plant Options

Even though they are both succulents, the stonecrop suffers in sustained periods of drought and the partridge breast aloe is sensitive to overwatering. Fortunately, you can prevent problems by replacing the finicky aloe with a versatile zebra haworthia. If you'd prefer to water less, replace the sea urchin stonecrop with a string of pearls plant (Senecio rowleyanus).

My mother always taught me that to be a successful artist, you have to make the painting match the couch. The art might be jarring and provocative, but unless it looks good in somebody's house, you're still a starving artist. Other than the fact that you're only matching your own couch, these artistic indoor gardens are no different. It's easy enough to match a tan paint swatch to your favorite painting, but finding plants in subtle colors like tan or sage is a lot more difficult . . . or so you'd think. Bromeliads and succulents are so incredibly diverse that I had no problem coming up with a perfect palette of muted colors and rippled patterns. The dappled tan queen's tears looks as if it were made for the recycled wood container, and the white stripes and striations of the stonecrop and aloe tie in nicely with the color of the echeveria sitting front and center. Look even more closely and it would even appear as if the staggered striations of the aloe are playing a duet with those of the wood container. Sometimes, however, looks aren't everything.

Unless you use one of the substitutions above, this is actually a fairly difficult and incompatible arrangement compared to the others in the book. The key to success is to let the soil dry out between watering—but not for too long. If you use a small container as I have, expect to remove offsets occasionally to keep the pot from getting too crowded—or just use a larger container and fill in the gaps between plants with a decorative mulch such as sand or stones. Drainage is another must when the partridge breast aloe is involved, so it's imperative that the container has a drainage hole to keep stagnant water from settling around the roots. If you're a chronic overwaterer, you can even surround the roots of the aloe with perlite to keep them dry.

Caribbean Breeze

LIGHT	MOISTURE	HUMIDITY
Sunny	Average	Average

Shopping List

- Large container
- Regular potting mix
- **A** 1 sea grape (*Coccoloba uvifera*)
- **B** 2 burn jelly plants (*Bulbine frutescens*)
- **C** 1 purple lantana (*Lantana montevidensis*)

Plant Options

*No sea grape? No problem! Just use a sun-tolerant palm instead. Date palms (*Phoenix spp.*) and Mediterranean fan palms (*Chamaerops humilis*) both capture the look of a sandy beach and also thrive in the same sun that those flowers crave. If you can't find burn jelly plant or purple lantana, use orange lantana (*Lantana camara*) instead.*

A Caribbean beach scene means a hammock strung between coconut palms to most people, but if you were to ask a well-seasoned traveler about the most memorable tree of the region, you'd probably get an earful about a splendid tree called the sea grape. It might not fit into the clichéd impressions granted courtesy of "Margaritaville" and pirate movies, but beaches from central Florida to the northern shores of South America can be recognized by the cheerful round leaves of sea grape trees lining the dunes. These trees are incredibly useful for a host of applications in the tropics: dense wood suitable for furniture and buildings; round dinner-plate-sized leaves so leathery and tough that they were once used as postcards; and sweet "grapes" that are used to make wine and jellies. While you're not likely to get grapes indoors, you can still enjoy the round apple green leaves and vivid red veins. To complete the look of a beach, I've planted a grassy looking succulent called a burn jelly plant. A purple lantana completes the look of a beach planting and contrasts nicely with those of the orange flowers of the burn jelly plant.

Sea grapes thrive in regular potting soil, though a topdressing of sand and shells is definitely a nice decorative touch. While they do bounce back from drought and don't require much fertilizer, providing a little extra care is well worth your while. Keep the potting mix moist and feed occasionally to keep them looking at their best. Prune the sea grape occasionally. To allow more room for the other plants, remove the lowest leaves and let it grow to the desired height before pinching out the growing tips. *Lantana* and *Bulbine* plants are both relatively carefree but will drop spent flowers regularly. For this reason, grow them outdoors where winds whisk away the fallen blooms, making cleanup literally a breeze, or be prepared to pick up after them.

Chocolate Truffle

LIGHT	MOISTURE	HUMIDITY
Bright	Average	Average to high

Shopping List

- **Extra-small container**
- **Regular potting mix**
- **(A) 2 earth stars** (*Cryptanthus* 'Pink Star')
- **(B) 1 peperomia** (*Peperomia caperata*)
- **(C) 2 peperomias** (*Peperomia* 'Bianco Verde')

Plant Options

The main appeal of this combo is the dark foliage, but if the peperomias aren't available, spring for more commonly sold houseplants such as the waffle plant (Hemigraphis *spp.) or aluminum plant* (Pilea)*. The* Cryptanthus *is easily replaced by a pink nerve plant* (Fittonia) *or polka dot plant* (Hypoestes)*, but be sure to keep the soil moist.*

Throughout this book I'll be combining plants in a paint-by-numbers fashion since there's no way to really mix plants together to make new colors like we could if we were mixing paint. Luckily plants can mix the colors together all by themselves. For example, let's see how the *Peperomia* 'Bianco Verde' in this planting mixes colors to form a nice chocolate brown color. An artist would know that to create the color brown all she has to do is combine the colors of red and green, and plants do just that. Look closely at the tiny leaved peperomia plant and you'll notice that the tops of the leaves are a dull dark green, while the stems and undersides are colored a rich burgundy. The red pigment helps the plant absorb the mostly green wavelengths of light on the rainforest floor, but for us the benefits are strictly ornamental. To see what I mean, look at the peperomias from a distance and notice how the hues of green and red mix together to form a deep mahogany brown! Hold the planter up against a dark-stained piece of furniture and see for yourself. Peperomias aren't the only plants with this nifty trick, though, and the brown stripes of the pink earth star are made in much the same way.

When mixing these colors together, plant the serrated-leaved earth stars last to avoid inadvertently slicing off the leaves of the brittle peperomia plants. The peperomias do better with a bit of humidity, so tuck this little container onto the kitchen or bathroom counter near a sink, where they'll benefit from the moist air. Allow the soil to dry between watering. Constantly wet soil will rot the stems of the peperomia plants, but letting the soil stay dry for too long will cause the stems to flop over. If the colors start to fade and revert to green, move the planter to a brighter location.

Coral Reef Madness

LIGHT	MOISTURE	HUMIDITY
Bright to sunny	Low	Low

Shopping List

- Cactus potting mix
- Decorative seashells and sea glass
- **(A)** 1 grafted cactus
  (*Gymnocalycium mihanovichii* f. *rubra*)
- **(B)** 4 earth stars (*Cryptanthus bromelioides tricolor*)
- **(C)** 1 coral mistletoe cactus (*Rhipsalis cereuscula*)
- **(D)** 1 red dragon plant (*Huernia schneideriana*)
- **(E)** 1 princess pine
  (*Crassula muscosa pseudolycopodiodes*)

Plant Options

There are many succulents that look as if they belong under the sea. Grafted crested Euphorbia *looks very much like brain corals, as does the monstrose cereus (*Cereus peruvianus *'Monstrosus'). Otherwise, choose succulents with colors and shapes that look decidedly "un-plantlike," avoiding anything that has obvious leaves to break the illusion.*

There is no style of interior décor that can't be enhanced by the addition of plants. My home's living room has a strong aquatic vibe with colors of aquamarine and coral red, so the typical leafy houseplants would have seemed out of place. Luckily for my wife and I, there are plants for every look. In this arrangement, earth stars resemble starfish more than plants, and divers might even compare them to coral polyps. The red dragon plant produces small burgundy flowers that also look like starfish, but when it isn't blooming, it resembles anything from a coral branch to a wandering tentacle. A purple grafted cactus could easily be mistaken for a sea urchin, at least until it blooms and produces vivid pink feathered flowers like the plumes of a colorful feather worm. To create the appearance of seafloor vegetation, I've included princess pine and coral mistletoe cactus. Stare long enough and they'll even appear to sway in the imaginary ocean currents. Place this container near an aquarium, in a nautically decorated room, or on the table as a centerpiece right next to the shrimp cocktail.

Caring for these denizens of the deep is much easier than maintaining a saltwater aquarium and it doesn't require much water at all. Because this bowl is shallow and the cactus mix drains quickly, you may need to water more often. If it dries out too quickly, replace using regular potting mix or add coir. Direct light isn't a necessity for this grouping, but it helps. The plants in the photograph had been growing without direct sunlight and still look attractive, but a sunny spot will give the earth stars brighter pink colors and keep the other plants tight and compact. The only plant that really requires direct light is the princess pine, because it would otherwise take on a lanky form and attract pests.

Coral Seafoam

LIGHT	MOISTURE	HUMIDITY
Sunny	Low	Low

Shopping List

- Medium to wide container
- Cactus potting mix
- Barnacle clump
- **(A)** 3 string of beans (*Senecio radicans glauca*)
- **(B)** 2 graptoveria (×*Graptoveria* 'Bashful')
- **(C)** 4 jelly bean plants (*Sedum rubrotinctum* 'Aurora')
- **(D)** 1 pink crassula (*Crassula marginalis rubra variegata*)
- **(E)** 2 pink mimicry plants
  (*Anacampseros telaphiastrum variegata*)
- **(F)** 1 echeveria (*Echeveria* 'Lola')

Plant Options

The best succulents for this container don't necessarily look like aquatic life on their own, but they do when grouped together. To get that coral reef effect, choose really colorful succulents with tightly clustered leaves such as Crassula, Echeveria, *and* Sedum *plants. They look great even without the barnacles!*

Often, the most impressive plants are the ones that look very little like plants at all. Hailing from dry plateaus, deserts, beaches, and even treetops, succulents have filled almost every possible niche with fleshy stems and leaves designed to hold water and blend in with their surroundings. The succulents used in this container look as if they're trying to blend in with the fiesta of a bustling coral reef. An addition of barnacles takes the arrangement just over the edge and into the sea, making the pink and seafoam colored succulents look even more aquatic. You can add other fun decorations, such as fish sculptures or a mulch of glass beads. If you are using seashells, coral, or barnacles, disinfect them thoroughly in a solution of bleach before rinsing and drying them in the shade. While I chose succulents with seafoam green and pink leaves to match the pot and barnacles, you're only limited by your garden center's selection and your imagination. Plant the trailing string of beans near the sides of the pot so that they can hang their banana-shaped leaves over the edge—not over other plants. The planter's low profile makes it an excellent choice for a creative tablescape, so serve it up alongside dinner when entertaining guests!

Pack the plants in as tightly as possible for the biggest impact, planting the mimicry plants in between larger succulents where they'll benefit from the shade. When the plants get overgrown, thin them by taking cuttings. To avoid getting potting mix on the succulents when planting, start from the sides and add small scoops of soil as you work. Give this container combo a bright and sunny spot where it can be enjoyed and water only once the soil has been allowed to dry out thoroughly.

Cubicle Buddy

LIGHT	MOISTURE	HUMIDITY
Low to bright	Average	Average to high

Shopping List

- Small container
- Regular potting mix
- (A) 1 bromeliad (*Vriesea sucrei* hybrid)
- (B) 2 Florida gold dracaenas
  (*Dracaena* 'Florida Gold')
- (C) 1 satin pothos (*Scindapsus pictus*)

Plant Options

If a purple-leaved bromeliad proves elusive, replace it with another upright purple plant such as one of these peacock plants: Calathea makoyana *or* Calathea insignis. *If you use either of these, be sure to keep the soil moist at all times. Satin pothos can be swapped out with another dark-leaved vine such as* Philodendron melanochrysum *or one of the vining peperomias.*

The Cubicle Buddy is the perfect co-worker. Content to patiently remove toxins from your workplace without any compensation or hopes for promotion, he remains in your shadow for nothing more than the occasional drink from the water cooler. You can even use the bromeliad's leaves to hold up important memos to co-workers (Do Not Disturb—Sleeping) or stash expense reports away so you have room to doodle, but it might just cost you a little monthly fertilizer for the privilege. Come on, plants have needs. When the bromeliad has been employed for three to five years, expect to see it get a raise in the form of a tall red flower spike with yellow flowers. After the promotion of a lifetime, the mother plant will begin her slow decline only to be replaced by baby bromeliads at the base, which will eventually take over running the business on her behalf.

The vivid contrasting colors of purple and chartreuse might seem a bit wild and irresponsible, but rest assured that everything about this container combo is efficient, right down to the square-shaped pot that fits snugly in a corner of your desk. Satin pothos hangs straight down until it cascades off your Formica desk, and the dracaenas form a leafy upright screen that frames the bromeliad and blocks the wandering gaze of your nosy co-worker. Just because she's your boss doesn't mean she gets to watch you play solitaire. With your new protégé, even watering is a breeze! Pour water in the center of the bromeliad's watertight cup until it dribbles out of the leaves enough to wet the soil. This will also flush out any excess salts caused by hard water. The satin pothos will eventually start to ramble around and trail off your desk, so keep it in its place by pruning extra-long shoots at the base. There's no need to feel guilty about the routine maintenance, because the workplace can be pretty competitive after all.

Dish Garden Redux

LIGHT	MOISTURE	HUMIDITY
Sunny	Low	Low

Shopping List

- Small container
- Cactus potting mix
- **A** 3 echeverias (*Echeveria* 'Lola')
- **B** 2 princess pines (*Crassula muscosa pseudolycopodiodes*)
- **C** 1 maraca plant (*Portulaca molokiniensis* 'Maraca')
- **D** 4 mini jelly bean plants (*Sedum rubrotinctum* 'Mini')
- **E** 1 haworthia (*Haworthia marumiana* v. *batesiana*)
- **F** 3 inch plants (*Tradescantia fluminensis*)
- **G** 2 string of bananas (*Senecio radicans*)

Plant Options

There's no way you'll manage to score all of these succulents on a single trip to the garden center, but there are many more that will give you the same look. Seek out succulents from the Echeveria, Sedum, *and* Portulacaria *genera with woody looking stems. Whatever succulents you use, be sure to remove the lower leaves to help them look a bit more like trees.*

The dish gardens usually offered for sale are horrible abominations of poor design and planning and usually feature a random scattering of incompatible plants in a bowl with absolutely no drainage. But when they're done right, dish gardens can be absolutely magical. Start by choosing plants that not only require the same conditions of direct sun and excellent drainage but also have harmonious colors and varied textures. Because real landscapes are overwhelmingly green, most of the plants chosen are also green. I've also used a handful of lavender-gray echeverias to add interest and echo the color of the bowl and made it a point to vary the plants' textures to complete the illusion of a tiny world. For the appearance of trees, simply remove the lower leaves of the *Echeveria* and *Portulaca*, and prune their tips to make them form branches.

Most miniature gardens need a lot of water and care, but this one can handle a considerable amount of neglect and requires only occasional pruning to keep the plants' bonsai-like forms. To best attain the appearance of a miniature landscape, divide and conquer. Divide the succulents before planting, allow the cuts to dry and heal for a day or two, and plant the divisions and cuttings to resemble a forest. Place taller succulents such as the *Echeveria* and *Portulaca* in the center for a natural look. Water one to two times a week during the growing season and sparingly in winter. The plants will survive long periods of drought but will look a lot better with regular watering. The inch plants and string of bananas plants require more pruning, but they will also cover empty patches while you wait for the slow growers to fill in.

Easy Breezy Bonsai

LIGHT	MOISTURE	HUMIDITY
Bright	Average	Average

Shopping List

- Medium container
- Regular potting mix
- Orchid bark
- Moss
- **A** 1 heavenly bamboo
  (*Nandina domestica* 'Gulf Stream')
- **B** 1 Walter's viburnum
  (*Viburnum obovatum*)
- **C** 1 dwarf mondo grass (*Ophiopogon japonica* 'Kyoto Dwarf')

Plant Options

*If you have a hard time finding the Walter's viburnum used here, there are lots of other small and bushy plants to take its place. Purchase a pre-made bonsai at the garden center or train one yourself. Umbrella tree (*Schefflera arboricola*) is a superb bonsai for indoors. The nandina is easily replaced by a Ming aralia or a false aralia.*

Bonsai gets a bad rap for being too difficult for the average gardener, but I beg to differ. With the right plants and a little bit of pruning every now and then, it's easy to grow a miniature landscape in the comfort of your own home. What makes it so charming, in my opinion, is the fine texture of each plant's leaves. Tiny leaves are hard to find in a houseplant, so it's worth a little extra effort to grow them whenever possible. Another way that this combination stands out is its use of negative space. Each plant is isolated from its neighbor by a mulch of orchid bark, making it look even more like a natural woodland floor. Nandina in its common form can outgrow a container quickly, but 'Gulf Stream', 'Firepower', and other colorful selections grow slowly enough that they can be maintained with little effort. Dwarf mondo grass isn't always included in houseplant books, but it has proven itself invaluable as a bonsai companion plant. Walter's viburnum is a bit of an anomaly because it's not usually sold as a houseplant, but it thrives in the same warm temperate climate as the other plants in the arrangement and has also been successfully grown as a bonsai.

The plants in this arrangement will thrive in a bright room, with or without direct light. If you do decide to move it to a sunny windowsill, do it slowly so that the plants have time to acclimate. Keep the soil moist at all times. These plants will be at their happiest if they're placed in a well-ventilated room that stays unheated in winter, and they can even tolerate hard freezes if inadvertently left outdoors! As the plants grow, prune them to shape by removing any long shoots, crossing branches, or suckers from the base. To maintain the tree-like appearance, remove lower leaves and branches as they appear.

The Executive

LIGHT	MOISTURE	HUMIDITY
Bright to sunny	Low	Low

Shopping List

- Extra-small container
- Cactus potting mix
- **A** 1 zebra haworthia (*Haworthia attenuata*)
- **B** 2 window leaf haworthia plants (*Haworthia obtusifolia*)
- **C** 1 cylindrical snake plant (*Sansevieria cylindrica*)
- **D** 1 tiger's jaws (*Faucaria tigrina*)
- **E** 1 gasteria plant (*Gasteria bicolor* var. *bicolor*)
- **F** 3 dwarf gasteria (*Gasteria bicolor* var. *liliputana*)

Plant Options

Think small for big results. Haworthia *and* Gasteria *plants are excellent choices for their neat and tidy clumping habit and shade tolerance, so stick to those unless you plan on getting a bigger pot. Alternately, other larger succulents may be grown as cuttings and pruned or removed when they get too large.*

Think outside the box and hit the ground running with this results-driven executive container combo. With their drought tolerance and diverse skill set, these plants will tough it out like a boss while you're busy getting results and making things happen. The window leaf haworthia's transparency makes it a trusted advisor, while the gasteria's stony demeanor reassures you that it will stay the course when everyone else is jumping ship. And because the best defense is a good offense, the little tiger's jaws plant is always at the ready to strike while the iron's hot. The big elephant in the room, however, is the imposing cylindrical snake plant: built on a narrow and economical footprint, yet robust enough to show everyone in the office that you're too big to fail. Impress colleagues and foreign investors with a horticultural metaphor or two from your new hobby to sound smart in confusing situations. Just say, "We need a strategy that's moisture retentive *and* has good drainage," and everyone around the table will nod in earnest agreement.

There's no need to worry about your bottom line with these efficient plants on your workforce, and they're incredibly productive despite the fact that they only need a weekly trip to the water cooler. Vacation time and health insurance won't be necessary, but they'd be willing to fall on their sword for you if they're assured that you'll give them plenty of room to grow. If the cylindrical snake plant starts to poke through the glass ceiling and becomes too top heavy, just repot it in a wider container. You will have to supervise the smaller succulents periodically to make sure that pests like scale insects aren't bringing down morale and give them a brighter window office if they start to look lean and lanky.

Femme Fatale

LIGHT	MOISTURE	HUMIDITY
Bright	Average	Average

Shopping List

- Small container
- Regular potting mix
- **Ⓐ** 1 pink dracaena
  (*Dracaena marginata* 'Colorama')
- **Ⓑ** 1 waffle plant (*Hemigraphis exotica*)
- **Ⓒ** 2 prayer plants (*Maranta tricolor*)
- **Ⓓ** 1 black philodendron
  (*Philodendron melanochrysum*)

Plant Options

To achieve this look with other plants, just look for other plants with black leaves. Peperomia 'Bianco Verde', aluminum plant (Pilea spp.), and black earth star (Cryptanthus zonatus) are all good fits. The dracaena in the center should be relatively easy to find, but it can also be started by cuttings from a larger plant or replaced with any other dracaena available.

Francis Bacon once said, "In order for the light to shine so brightly, the darkness must be present." When I was a brooding teenage goth, I would have used this quote to justify my antisocial behavior and wardrobe of black boots and trenchcoats. As a bad teenage poet, I also hoped that it would make me appear more intellectual. To celebrate the inherent rebellious nature of a color that refuses to be defined as a color at all (technically, black is the result of the absence of color or a combination of all colors), I've taken some of the most commonly combined houseplants and brought them together to suffer in the dark and eternal embrace of a wicked matte black container. The so-called purple waffle plant has now been claimed by the night and seems to have embraced its darkness, and the satin locks of a black philodendron tumble down into the abyss like the raven hair of a vampire vixen. A neon pink spike of dracaena stabs through the arrangement, adding a bit of allure and excitement to an otherwise dull scene. Even the prayer plant seems to have gone on a rebellious streak. The herringbone arrangement of blood red veins across each leaf would have gone unnoticed in a more wholesome setting, but now they seem more prominent and alluring than ever before. In order for these plants to shine so brightly, the darkness must also be present.

You'll need some bright indirect light and a bit of humidity present as well if you want them to thrive for all eternity. Repot or divide them when the pot gets too crowded, or just remove any unattractive stems. If you're moving up to a larger container and are really finding it hard to give up the little black pot, just divide the container and remove a couple of plants to create more growing space. If the plants lose their bright colors or revert to green, move them to a brighter location.

Fishtails and Feathers

LIGHT	MOISTURE	HUMIDITY
Low to bright	Average to high	Average to high

Shopping List

- Large container
- Regular potting mix
- Coir
- **A** 1 pinstripe plant
  (*Calathea majestica albolineata*)
- **B** 2 purple calathea plants
  (*Calathea roseopicta* 'Dottie')
- **C** 1 tuna tail palm (*Chamaedorea metallica*)
- **D** 2 English ivies (*Hedera helix* 'Mona Lisa')

Plant Options

The tuna tail palm is the namesake of this recipe, but it is easily replaced with another small palm (Chamaedoria spp.) or a peace lily. To get a similar look without the purple calatheas, use another peacock plant (Maranta or Calathea) or waffle plant (Hemigraphis). English ivy could be replaced by a spikemoss (Selaginella) or another vining plant.

This is for the connoisseur who refuses to grow commonplace prayer plants and parlor palms but instead requires the exquisite beauty of their refined relatives. Tuna tail palm is a cumbersome and comical sounding name for what is perhaps the most elegant palm tree you could grow indoors. With shimmering sage leaves that appear to be gilded with a silver lining, its Latin name of *Chamaedorea metallica* is far more telling. *Chamaedorea* is whimsically translated as "near the ground gifts" because the plants are low growing and could indeed be considered gifts, and *metallica* obviously refers to the finish. The calatheas are also spectacular, and make their cousins in the *Maranta* genus look downright tacky and uncouth. The pinstripe plant does indeed have pinstripes, but rather than the fine lines you'd see on a suit, the elegant white lines look as if they've been painted painstakingly by hand. To each side you'll find the voluptuous *Calathea roseopicta* 'Dottie' with leaves of royal purple and rose highlighting the silvery centerpieces, and classy English ivies at their base are at the ready like well-paid servants.

These superior specimens might command a higher price tag and definitely need a posh environment of humidity and constantly moist soil but are entirely worth it. Place this arrangement in a conservatory or by a claw-footed bathtub in a well-lit bathroom, or bring it outdoors to the shade where it can bask in the warm moisture of the summer air. Remove dead lower leaves as they appear and periodically clean the leaves to prevent spider mites and thrips, which proliferate in dry air. To their sophisticated palates, a regular feeding of a balanced houseplant fertilizer is as precious as fine caviar. When the calatheas have begun to crowd the pot, thin their stems and remove the ivies.

Flavor Trippin'

LIGHT	MOISTURE	HUMIDITY
Bright	High	High

Shopping List

- Medium container
- Regular potting mix
- Coir or peat moss
- **A** 1 miracle fruit (*Synsepalum dulcificum*)
- **B** 3 spikemosses (*Selaginella* spp.)
- **C** 2 nerve plants
  (*Fittonia argyroneura* 'Pink Vein')
- **D** 1 orthophytum plants
  (*Orthophytum saxicola*)
- **E** 1 Fiji hare's foot fern (*Davallia feejensis*)

Plant Options

*There's no replacement for the magical miracles of miracle fruit, but you can use another houseplant with a tree form and small leaves to get the same look. Weeping fig (*Ficus benjamina*), false aralia (*Schefflera elegantissima*), and dwarf umbrella tree (*Schefflera arboricola*) are all good alternatives. Other good fruit trees for indoors include dwarf citrus trees, starfruit (*Averrhoa carambola*), and pomegranates (*Punica granatum*).*

Come closer. If you can promise me that you won't tell anybody about what you see here, I'll give you some magical berries that will blow your ever-loving mind and alter your reality. These "miracle berries" make sour things taste sweet. Don't believe me? Pop one of these in your mouth, eat a lemon, and try not to freak out. Here's how all this weird science works: The miraculin substance in the fruit are glycoprotein molecules that stick to taste buds and activate the sweet receptors, thus tricking us into thinking that acidic and sour foods are actually sweet! Freaky, huh? It's been used medicinally and recreationally in Africa for centuries, but only recently has it started to catch on in the United States. When the FDA classified it as a food additive instead of a sweetener back in the '70s, miraculin was forced to take a back seat to sugar and other sweeteners. It's a real bummer too, because miracle fruit actually has a low sugar content and shows a lot of promise as a healthier sugar substitute.

It gets better. Miracle fruit is actually very easy to grow indoors and doesn't need the direct light that's required by most fruits and herbs. Here's how you can keep them healthy: Miracle fruit drinks a lot of water and needs constant moisture, so mix coir or peat moss into your potting mix in a 1:3 ratio. If the surrounding nerve plants and spikemosses start looking limp, that's your cue to get the watering can, ASAP. When planting the spikemosses, pin down the stems to help get their roots started. Mist each plant in the combo every one to two days to raise the humidity and dislodge any pests. Place the container by a well-lit kitchen sink both for humidity and to have a freshly grown sweetener at the ready.

Flower Shop Delight

LIGHT	MOISTURE	HUMIDITY
Bright	High	High

Shopping List

- Medium container (wide azalea pot)
- Regular potting mix
- Vermiculite, orchid mix, or another free-draining amendment
- **A** 1 flamingo lily (*Anthurium andreanum*)
- **B** 1 arrowhead vine (*Syngonium podophyllum* 'White Butterfly')
- **C** 2 gold spikemosses (*Selaginella kraussiana* 'Aurea')
- **D** 2 nerve plants (*Fittonia argyroneura* 'Pink Vein')

Plant Options

These are all relatively common, yet with the exception of the arrowhead vine, they can be difficult to grow. If you're unable to provide the humidity they require, swap out with less finicky plants. Creeping fig (Ficus pumila) *has an aggressive root system but is a much tougher alternative to the spikemoss groundcover. Replace the anthurium with a durable Chinese evergreen* (Aglaonema spp.) *or a dumb cane* (Dieffenbachia spp.).

I told you to steer clear of finicky plants when making mixed plantings, but with the right care, some plants prove to be worth the extra trouble. I also warned that you should be careful when planting tall plants in short containers, lest you end up with a top-heavy concoction that looks more like a flower arrangement than a proper container garden. But that isn't necessarily a bad thing, and a living arrangement of compatible houseplants sure beats the go-to gift of a dozen dead roses. The anthurium makes a natural choice for a living flower arrangement because the flowers can be clipped for display elsewhere in the home. Spikemoss creeps over the edge of the pot and lends a weathered look, while the red-veined nerve plants add a dash of color.

Give these plants ample warmth, drainage, moisture, and humidity. Add an amendment such as vermiculite to the potting mix in a 1:5 ratio so that the anthurium roots have room to breathe, and mist them daily. To keep the rapidly growing arrowhead vine in check, cut the stems to the base in spring and remove divisions with a sharp, clean knife. Nerve plants and spikemosses are notorious for mysteriously dying overnight if the soil dries out, so it's best to view them as temporary plants that can be replaced. If the plants develop crispy brown edges on their leaves, move them to a humid location such as the kitchen, or just spray with a fine mist periodically. If the leaves of the anthurium begin to turn pale, it's time to start feeding with a general houseplant fertilizer. Compost tea works well and is less likely to burn the roots and foliage of the spikemosses.

High Fashion

LIGHT	MOISTURE	HUMIDITY
Sunny	Low to average	Low

Shopping List

- Medium container
- Regular potting mix
- **(A)** 1 queen's tears
  (*Billbergia hoelscheriana*)
- **(B)** 1 graptosedum (×*Graptosedum*)
- **(C)** 3 sorrel plants (*Oxalis spiralis* subsp.
  vulcanicola 'Plum Crazy Yellow')
- **(D)** 4 echeverias
  (*Echeveria* 'Topsy Turvy')

Plant Options

Other sorrels without a weedy habit include Oxalis triangularis *'Atropurpurea' with purple leaves,* Oxalis *'Sunshine Velvet' with golden leaves, and* Oxalis *'Burgundy Bliss' with burgundy leaves and contrasting yellow flowers. The* Graptosedum *and* Echeveria *plants can be replaced by* Graptopetalum paraguayense, Kalanchoe tomentosa, *or any other gray succulents that form a flower shape with their leaves.*

Indoor gardens are indeed fashionable, but this one seems poised to take over the runways with a ravishing silhouette of succulents against the velvety texture of sorrels. Succulent and cacti growers are all too familiar with seeing the shamrock-shaped leaves of the weedy *Oxalis stricta* popping up between spines and making weeding a dangerous proposition, but not all *Oxalis* plants are bad. The deep wine-colored-leaved cultivar 'Plum Crazy Yellow' is a different breed altogether and actually thrives alongside succulents without getting weedy! The result is a high-fashion ensemble resembling a modern floral print, with the gray silhouettes of the flower-shaped succulents standing out dramatically against the richly dark magenta backdrop of sorrels. One narrow queen's tears adds height to the design, complements the succulents, and contrasts nicely with the deep and vivid color of the sorrel. Try this design out on a sunny bedroom dresser where it will inspire your wardrobe for the day, or place it against a bright yellow wall where the sorrel's cheery flowers come into their own. If your room is modern and sleek, use a polished ceramic or fiberglass pot in white, gray, or yellow. For more traditional décor, use terracotta or cast iron.

When planting, add the sorrels first and the succulents last to avoid breaking their brittle stems. Keep the soil lightly moist from spring through fall, allowing it to dry out between watering in winter. If you plant larger succulents like the *Echeveria* 'Topsy Turvy' used here, prepare to thin them out when they grow up so that they don't overtake the other plants. Remove offsets as needed so that they don't smother the sorrels, but be sure to at least let one of the echeverias get to blooming size. Their tall and arching stems appear as if they were decorated by fondant petals, and the flowers open up to a glowing peachy orange hue.

Hot Pink Limeade

LIGHT	MOISTURE	HUMIDITY
Bright	Average	Average

Shopping List

- Extra-large container
- Regular potting mix
- **(A)** 1 pink bromeliad (*Neoregelia* 'Sexy Pink')
- **(B)** 2 wax plants (*Hoya carnosa*)
- **(C)** 2 peperomias (*Peperomia* 'Rainbow')
- **(D)** 1 dracaena (*Dracaena deremensis* 'Limelight')
- **(E)** 1 dracaena (*Dracaena deremensis* 'Lemon Lime')
- **(F)** 1 Chinese evergreen (*Aglaonema* 'Siam Aurora')

Plant Options

Any bromeliad would make a suitable replacement for the Neoregelia *'Sexy Pink', especially* Aechmea fasciata *with its pink flowers and white powdered leaves. If the red aglaonema is unavailable, use a lime green dieffenbachia. You can also substitute pothos or a vining peperomia for the wax vine or use* Dracaena marginata *in place of the peperomia.*

If ever there were a container combo for the chic and stylish uptown girl, Hot Pink Limeade is a girl's best friend. Waxy pink and lime green foliage brings on the glam like luscious pink lips and candy-coated fingernails, while the wax vine drapes down sparsely like a delicate necklace. The beauty of this ensemble is that it stays attractive and never seems to show its age. As the dracaenas grow taller, the peperomia and bromeliads fill in to form a full and attractive wall of foliage.

What better star for this fashion show than a blushing bromeliad by the name of *Neoregelia* 'Sexy Pink'? Even when out of bloom, this stunner keeps her gorgeous color year-round. *Peperomia magnoliifolia* 'Rainbow' repeats the same hue on the edges of its succulent leaves, but the leaves' frosty white undersides mirror the color of the container. *Dracaena deremensis* 'Lemon Lime' and 'Limelight' provide a lush and upright backdrop of lime green, while the trailing deep green leaves of wax vine provide deep shadows and stark contrast against the container.

You would have to forget about this container for a long time for it to die of drought, but it will look a whole lot nicer with proper care. Water well when the soil has become dry, and fill the bromeliad's cup with water when empty. The wax vine and peperomia may become overgrown but can easily be kept in bounds with occasional pruning. With clean, sharp pruners, prune the oldest stems back to the ground or back to the point right above where the leaves meet the stem. Bromeliads die back after blooming, but are soon replaced by "pups" or plantlets that form at the base. Once the new plantlets have reached half the size of the original rosette, remove the declining portion with pruners or with a vigorous twist of the hand.

An Indoor Flowerbed

LIGHT	MOISTURE	HUMIDITY
Bright to sunny	Average	Average

Shopping List

- Large container
- Regular potting mix
- **(A)** 1 variegated shell ginger
  (*Alpinia zerumbet* 'Variegata')
- **(B)** 3 wax begonias (*Begonia semperflorens*)
- **(C)** 2 coleus plants (*Coleus blumei*)

Plant Options

*There are lots of other plants sold as annuals that will do well indoors, especially if you're willing to replace them as they decline. Here are a few to seek out: caladiums, heliconias, New Guinea impatiens, polka dot plant (*Hypoestes *cv.), and hidden ginger (*Curcuma *spp.) are all relatively easy to find at the garden center.*

Are all those houseplants starting to take a toll on your wallet? Then step away from the houseplant section of your garden center and look among the annual bedding plants for some real steals. The plants in this container rang up at a grand total of about ten bucks, and the pot was just repurposed from a neglected *Ficus* tree planting. If you're looking for other annuals to use in indoor arrangements, choose tropical ones that can handle a bit of shade. Wax begonias and coleus both come in a variety of colors and can be found at a bargain in cell trays, sold in 4-inch pots or even in large 1-gallon containers. Mass them as a bedding plant around a focal point as I've done here, or tuck them in other plantings while you're waiting for slower-growing plants to fill out. Focal points like this variegated shell ginger can be found affordably as a summer annual if you time your shopping just right, and I have even found exotic plants such as heliconias and pineapple lilies hiding amongst the marigolds. Annuals aren't always the best candidates for living indoors, but if the price is right, why not take a chance?

Outdoors you should put these plants in a shadier part of the garden, but indoors they do best in an east- or west-facing window that receives direct sunlight in the morning or afternoon. Provide enough water to keep the compost evenly moist at all times, and leave a gap in your planting scheme (as I have) so that you can easily check on the moisture levels. When planting the begonias, take care not to damage the brittle leaves, and remove unsightly spent flowers as needed. Variegated shell ginger can grow quite large if given enough time, water, and humidity, but the tallest stems can be removed at the base to keep it at a manageable size. Bleached leaves on the ginger indicate sunburn, so move it to a spot out of direct light.

Ivy League

LIGHT	MOISTURE	HUMIDITY
Bright	Average	Average to high

Shopping List

- Large container
- Regular potting mix
- **(A)** 1 fatshedera (*Fatshedera lizei*)
- **(B)** 2 English ivies (*Hedera helix* 'Mona Lisa')
- **(C)** 2 Algerian ivies (*Hedera canariensis* 'Gloire de Marengo')

Plant Options

Ivies are this combo's claim to fame, but they are also very easy to find. Any English ivy will make a suitable replacement for the two ivies at the base, and a creeping fig will also make a suitable replacement. The fatshedera can be switched out with the related Japanese aralia (Fatsia japonica) or a Buddhist pine (Podocarpus).

Few houseplants can convincingly capture the feel of the great outdoors better than ivies, and you'll be hard pressed to find a plant so well suited to adding a touch of class and tradition to container gardens. This grouping combines the best of the best, from the little filigreed leaves of the 'Mona Lisa' to the statuesque fatshedera. There are countless English ivy cultivars from which to choose, but the finely divided and variegated cultivars are the most distinctive in arrangements and prove to be very useful as a spiller or groundcover at the base of other plants. The middle child in this family is the 'Gloire de Marengo' Algerian ivy, but the bright white variegation of its leaves help it stand out in defiance. The fatshedera is not really an ivy, but an intergeneric hybrid between *Fatsia japonica* and *Hedera helix*. To put it in layman's terms, fatshedera was a lovechild between the Japanese fatsia and the English ivy conceived at a French nursery in 1912. How's that for a story?

There are only eleven species of ivy, yet they're some of the most instantly recognizable plants around and are found naturally almost anywhere in Europe. English ivies grow so well outside their habitat that they've become weeds in the Pacific Northwest and other locales. Indoors, on the other hand, they need humidity, moisture, and indirect light to thrive. Keep the soil moist (but never soggy) at all times, and provide humidity if the leaf tips turn brown. If the vines seem lanky or the variegated markings revert back to green, slowly move the planter to a brighter spot. Prune as needed, taking care to avoid the irritating sap. To keep the fatshedera upright, tie it to a stake inserted into the mix. Ivies are often plagued by mealybugs if their requirements of moist soil and bright light aren't met, so inspect the base of each leaf for white fluffy insects periodically. Remove them by hand or with a good rinse.

Jungle Glow

LIGHT	MOISTURE	HUMIDITY
Bright	Average to high	Average to high

Shopping List

- Medium container
- Regular potting mix
- **A** 1 dracaena (*Dracaena* 'Limelight')
- **B** 2 lanceleaf rattlesnake plants (*Calathea lancifolia*)
- **C** 1 waffle plant (*Hemigraphis* cvv.)
- **D** 1 false aralia (*Schefflera elegantissima*)
- **E** 2 wandering Jew plants (*Tradescantia zebrina*)

Plant Options

For a more durable grouping, just replace the fussier waffle plant with a black philodendron (Philodendron melanochrysum) *or use another one of the plant choices in its place.* Dracaena deremensis *'Limelight' has glowing chartreuse foliage that is hard to beat, but* Dracaena *'Lemon Lime' and* Dracaena fragrans lindenii *come pretty close.*

Like moonlight through a dark and impenetrable jungle, *Dracaena* 'Limelight' stands out as a beacon against midnight hues of black, purple, and deep green. Jungle Glow is a study in restraint, with all of the plants working together to fade into an intricately woven textural backdrop so that the bright green dracaena can take center stage. The dark plants seem to blend into obscurity, but they only serve to give the whole grouping a greater impact. Even the black and brown container seems to work in tandem to show off the dracaena. At the rear, the peacock patterned leaves of the lanceleaf rattlesnake plant fold up every night, revealing their purple undersides and contrasting against the dracaena to dramatic effect. Apart from working well together aesthetically, these plants will also make a great team as they grow up together and fill out their space. As the dracaena rockets up above the other plants, the dark and feathery false aralia will follow suit and provide contrasting dark foliage in the long run. Purple waffle plants and wandering Jews clamber over the edge, softly blurring the boundary between the container and the planting. However, if they get too rambunctious and start to swallow the pot whole, just trim them back.

Care is easy provided the soil doesn't dry out and there's at least a little bit of humidity. The waffle plant and false aralia benefit from the extra humidity provided by their surrounding plants when small but might need more when they grow away from the shelter of the other plants. Leave a gap in the planting so that you can easily check the soil moisture and water when the top layer has become dry. The leaves of the waffle plant and false aralia may develop crispy brown tips in winter when the house's humidity is lowest, but they will quickly recover if the container is brought to a shady spot outdoors after the risk of frost.

Jurassic Spark

LIGHT	MOISTURE	HUMIDITY
Bright to sunny	Low	Low

Shopping List

- Large container
- Cactus potting mix
- **(A)** 1 ZZ plant (*Zamioculcas zamifolia*)
- **(B)** 3 bird's nest snake plants (*Sansevieria hahnii*)
- **(C)** 3 Gollum jade plants (*Crassula* 'Gollum')
- **(D)** 6 gasterias (*Gasteria* spp.)

Plant Options

Do you wish this recipe would work in a dim room? Just replace the gasterias and Gollum jade plants with bromeliads, mistletoe cacti, or more snake plants for an indoor garden that tolerates low light and occasional drought with ease. You can also swap out the ZZ plant with a taller snake plant.

I hope that I always hold onto the sense of wonder that I had growing up, back when I would daydream about riding dinosaurs around the elementary school, grasping onto the neck of a brachiosaurus and escaping into a world filled with possibility. On second thought, that was college. If you'd rather celebrate your youthful imagination in more discrete ways, you could always plant an indoor garden with just as much potential for imaginative wanderings as your old collection of plastic dino toys. Get through the workday by looking at the dorsal plates of your ZZ plant and fantasize about taking a ride on the leathery sails of a stegosaurus, or look deep into the bird's nest snake plant for a stolen glimpse of their roots—which look precisely like unhatched reptile eggs. The stubby "fingers" of Gollum jade appear to reach out like E.T. phoning home, and the reptilian *Gasteria* plants below almost seem to move around in the corner of your eye. This container combo is sure to be a smash hit for kids, so be sure to leave a little room for some toy dinosaurs of their own.

These plants will survive in the event of both catastrophic drought and smothering shade, enduring conditions that would drive a dinosaur extinct. Leave some of the ZZ plant's huge egg-like roots exposed above the soil line to give guests a double take when they lean in for a closer look. The Gollum jade plants will eventually grow stems and take on the appearance of a bonsai grown by Dr. Seuss—that is, unless you choose to prune them and keep them short and bushy. Both the snake plants and gasterias will begin to spread and fill out the pot if left unchecked, but you can remove offsets with a sharp knife to free up space and start new plants. Fertilizer is not absolutely necessary, but a light feeding every few months will improve their health and appearance.

Lavender Lullaby

LIGHT	MOISTURE	HUMIDITY
Sunny	Low	Low

Shopping List

- Medium container
- Cactus potting mix
- **A** 1 aeonium
  (*Aeonium arboreum atropurpureum*)
- **B** 2 wandering Jew plants
  (*Tradescantia zebrina*)
- **C** 2 graptosedum plants
  (×*Graptosedum* 'Darley Sunshine')
- **D** 3 mother of thousands plants (*Kalanchoe daigremontiana*)

Plant Options

Use a burgundy-colored Dyckia *plant as a replacement for the* Aeonium, *or select a purple-leaved* Echeveria *such as 'Afterglow'. Most gray-colored rosette-forming succulents will fit in just fine with this combo, particularly the lavender-hued ones.* Graptoveria *'Fred Ives',* Echeveria *'Purple Pearl', and* Echeveria *'Perle von Nuremburg' are all worth seeking out.*

Sometimes the only way I'm able to fall asleep at night is by counting not sheep, but plants. I'll start out feverishly rattling off all the plants I want to grow, but before long I begin to forget their names and start losing count before my eyes grow heavy and I fall asleep so I can dream about more plants. It sounds crazy, but if you tried to remember names like *Aeonium arboretum atropurpureum* and *Kalanchoe daigremontiana*, you'd start getting pretty sleepy too! Of course it helps when the plants I envision in my mind's eye are as fascinatingly dreamy as the ones used here. Aeonium's spiraling pinwheel-shaped rosettes are positively trippy-looking, and the mother of thousands seems more like a never-ending fractal of psychedelic patterns. Along the margins of each dappled leaf, multitudes of tiny new plants are born so that they can fall off and begin life anew somewhere else. A friend of mine had these as a weed in her yard but would never think to call them anything so harsh, as they were her favorite plants. Nonetheless, avoid planting a mother of thousands plant if you're concerned about it turning up in your other potted cacti or succulents.

Place these succulents in an unobstructed south-facing window where they'll receive plenty of direct light. To get even darker leaves on the *Aeonium*, bring the planter outdoors in summer so that it can soak up the sun like a sunflower would. Take care when planting the wandering Jew, as the stems are very brittle. When a few stems inevitably fall off, just tuck them back into the soil where they'll put out new roots and grow. Water deeply so that moisture reaches the bottom of the pot, and allow the top layer of soil to dry out before watering again.

Lime and Coconut

LIGHT	MOISTURE	HUMIDITY
Bright	Average	Average to high

Shopping List

- Small container
- Regular potting mix
- **A** 1 ornamental pineapple (*Ananus lucidus*)
- **B** 1 peperomia (*Peperomia caperata*)
- **C** 1 peperomia (*Peperomia* 'Bianco Verde')
- **D** 1 pink earth star
  (*Cryptanthus* 'Pink Star')
- **E** 3 ivy plants (*Hedera helix*)

Plant Options

Most of the plants in this combo are easy to find and can be replaced by one of the many other peperomias or earth stars. If you can't find the ornamental pineapple, replace it with a spider plant (Chlorophytum comosum)*, a tricolor dracaena* (Dracaena marginata)*, or a bromeliad. Dracaena hybrids like 'Lemon Lime' and 'Limelight' both sound and look great too!*

I have a bad habit of ridiculing scented candles and beauty products for their misleading names. "Hibiscus Dream," I sneer, pointing at the candle. "Hibiscus doesn't even have a scent!" By the time I pick up the so-called "Beachtime Breeze" candle and prepare my retort about how the ocean *really* smells, my audience has moved on to the checkout counter with a basket stocked with "Newborn Baby" and "Blissful Dream" candles. One can only hope that they smell nothing like their namesakes. My own Lime and Coconut recipe is no different, and unless you light it on fire like a candle (which I wouldn't recommend), it's blissfully free of fragrance. But doesn't it make you think of a tropical escape where you're handed margaritas in halved coconut shells while listening to the sounds of marimbas and lapping waves? Lime green-colored ivies seem to glow against a backdrop of the coconut-brown peperomias, and a spectacular ornamental pineapple embraces the whole arrangement with its dark and arching leaves.

Eventually the pineapple will form a tiny pink fruit, looking much like the pineapples in the grocery store, but much smaller and prettier. While it's probably best to enjoy it on the plant, it can be eaten. Just make sure you use an equally tiny knife. After flowering and fruiting, the pineapple plant will produce offsets (babies) that can be divided by following the tips on page 37. Because ivies are usually sold as several rooted cuttings in a single container, they can be divided and planted separately along the edge of the pot for an attractive ring of bright foliage. Care is pretty straightforward, but give them humidity for the best results.

A Living Wreath

LIGHT	MOISTURE	HUMIDITY
Bright to sunny	Epiphytic	Average to high

Shopping List

- Grapevine wreath
- Wire or hot glue
- Decorative moss
- **A** 5 air plants (*Tillandsia ionatha*)
- **B** 1 curly air plant (*Tillandsia intermedia*)
- **C** 1 air plant (*Tillandsia tenuifolia*)
- **D** 1 hard leaf air plant (*Tillandsia stricta*)
- **E** 1 fuzzy air plant (*Tillandsia tectorum*)
- **F** 1 air plant (*Tillandsia xerografica*)
- **G** 1 bromeliad (*Vriesea corcovadensis*)

Plant Options

There's no need to look for the exact Tillandsia *species used here, as almost any of them will work well for this project. However, keep in mind that those with silver leaves are much more drought tolerant than those with green leaves. They get their silvery appearance from specialized cells called trichomes, which allow them to more efficiently harvest moisture from the air. Another plant to look for is the vining* Dischidia nummularioides, *also called string of coins.*

Don't let the elegant look of this living wreath fool you. It's just as easy to plant as any of the other container combinations in this book, and care is as simple as providing a weekly spritz of water. Best of all, unlike the messy evergreen wreaths to which you've grown accustomed, this living wreath will provide greenery and flowers throughout the year and can be re-used for years to come. Hang the wreath on the wall, or start some conversations by laying it flat on the table to serve as a marvelous candlelit centerpiece. You can adorn it with bows or ribbons for the holidays and toss them out when the season is over, but don't ditch the wreath just yet. Simply remove the bows and enjoy the sporadic blooms of the air plants all year long. Air plants all have very similar requirements, and your garden center might even have a different selection from which to choose. If they're not in stock, purchase from one of the websites on page 170.

To attach the *Tillandsia* plants, gently string wire through the lower leaves and then lace it through the gaps of the grapevine wreath. Tie the wire off tightly to secure the plant. Alternately, use a hot glue gun to apply a dab near the center of each *Tillandsia*'s base, and attach them to the wreath. Conceal the wire with decorative moss or Spanish moss (which is also a type of *Tillandsia*) and then add decorations of your choosing. To water the *Tillandsia* plants, spray them with a mister once every one to two weeks. Feed them by adding water-soluble orchid food to the water according to label instructions. If your house is especially low in humidity, choose *Tillandsia* with silvery leaves over those with green ones.

Middle Earth

LIGHT	MOISTURE	HUMIDITY
Bright to sunny	Low	Low

Shopping List

- Large container
- Cactus potting mix
- **A** 1 Gollum jade plant (*Crassula* 'Gollum')
- **B** 2 drunkard's dream (*Hatiora salicornoides*)
- **C** 6 window-leaved haworthia plants (*Haworthia* spp.)

Plant Options

If you can bear to part with the Gollum jade's cool name, replace it with any other jade plant for a similar look. Other succulents with a tree-like form include Portulaca molokiniensis *'Maraca' and* princess pine (Crassula muscosa). *If the grouping will get lots of direct light, the* Haworthia *plants can be switched out with echeverias or succulent peperomias.*

Escape from the dreariness of your workday by stepping into a magical realm upon your very desk, a little Middle-earth brimming with adventure and possibility. Use your imagination, and suddenly a story unfolds and draws you into its pages. A contorted 'Gollum' jade plant eagerly peers over a thicket of drunkard's dream cactus and translucent window plants in search of something that it seems to have lost long ago. The Gollum in our story might take on the appearance of a twisted bonsai tree, but it was once nothing more than a common jade plant, before the round succulent leaves mutated into frail and bony green fingers, always reaching and searching for . . . the *"precious."* Some of you Tolkien fans might want to slip an elvish ring of power onto one of Gollum's fingers, and hardcore Halflings would find it hard to resist tucking a scale replica of a Hobbit hole into the diorama. I chose a deep rectangular ceramic planter to highlight the backlit haworthias and flattened canopy of the jade tree, but a rustic container made of earthenware, stone, or wood would make the fantasy theme even more authentic.

These shade-tolerant succulents are durable enough to thrive in the forbidding land of Mordor through darkness and neglect, but they'll do best in bright light and water at least once a week. For the 'Gollum' jade plant, you can either start with a full-grown specimen or use a small one in a 4-inch pot. All of those fleshy little fingers can get quite heavy in time, so slip a couple of stakes or skewers in between the roots to hold it in place. The window-leaved haworthia plants will eventually produce offsets that billow out over the container's edge. Either remove and root the offsets by following the instructions on page 38 or allow them to keep growing like a mushroom cap to give the impression of eternal age.

Miniature Herb Garden

LIGHT	MOISTURE	HUMIDITY
Sunny	Average	Average

Shopping List

- Small container
- Regular potting mix
- (A) 1 rosemary (*Rosmarinus officinalis*)
- (B) 4 assorted thyme plants (*Thymus* cv.)

Plant Options

With so many thymes and rosemary plants from which to choose, who can decide? Thymus vulgaris *is the common English thyme, but there are many others such as lemon thyme, creeping thyme, and French thyme. The commonly grown* Rosmarinus officinalis *can grow to 2–4 feet tall unless pruned, but the 'Roman Beauty' cultivar gets my pick for its bushy dwarf habit.*

For those of you who want it all, I've brought two of the coolest gardening trends together in a single bowl: miniature gardens and edibles! To transform a bunch of ordinary herbs into a tiny land of tasty trees and savory shrubs, all I had to do was choose the right container and add some decorative mulch. I chose the stony bowl to impart a warm and sun-baked Mediterranean feel to the design. The gravel was suggested by a helpful garden center associate who collected some from right off of the ground. The result was a natural looking planting that somehow appears as if it had been growing for years. As you prune each plant to attain an aged bonsai-like look, don't forget to add the clippings of the savory herbs to your food! Use thyme to flavor meats, seafood, and stocks, and wrap rosemary around chicken breasts or pork tenderloins before cooking. Display this arrangement on the kitchen windowsill or on the table in a sunny dining room where it can be used while cooking or eating dinner.

To give the thyme and rosemary plants a tree-like habit, remove the lower branches and leaves to make trunks. To make them bushy, prune them in the same way you would clip a hedge. Water the plants thoroughly each time but do not allow the potting mix to stay soggy. Most pests can be treated by running the container under the faucet, but for serious infestations, spray with insecticidal soap and thoroughly rinse the solution off with water afterward. Swap out the plants as they decline (or are eaten) with vigorous new specimens or root cuttings to replace them for free. You can also find new plants or cuttings at the grocery store, but be sure to move them into the sun slowly so they don't burn. If you notice that the plant isn't growing as vigorously or that the leaves are turning yellow, feed with a balanced fertilizer according to label instructions.

Mossy Falls

LIGHT	MOISTURE	HUMIDITY
Bright	High	High

Shopping List

- Large container
- Regular potting mix
- Coir or peat
- **A** 1 stromanthe (*Stromanthe sanguinea*)
- **B** 1 spider plant (*Chlorophytum comosum*)
- **C** 1 mistletoe cactus (*Rhipsalis* spp.)
- **D** 2 waffle plants (*Hemigraphis*)

Plant Options

If stromanthe is unavailable, swap it out with a tall peacock plant such as Calathea lancifolia *or* Calathea ornata. *A rubber plant (*Ficus decora*) also makes a beautiful substitution, and it's common as well. Any* Rhipsalis *will work well as a spiller, but if they're unavailable, just use a vining peperomia or philodendron instead.*

The strange noises began right after I planted this container with a deep green and eggplant-colored stromanthe and sat it by the window. Every evening like clockwork my wife and I would hear a loud rustling across the living room and the blinds would then sway on their own accord, giving us reason to think that an animal was stowed away in a houseplant, seeking a warmer winter home. It was only after something like the tenth or thirteenth time that I realized that it wasn't an animal making the racket, but the plant itself! The stromanthe has the same bedtime habit of closing up its leaves at night to conserve water as its prayer plant relatives, but it's just a lot more noticeable because it's a large plant and makes a lot more noise. So there you have it: the stromanthe is a big purple plant that moves on its own and makes a lot of noise. Who needs pets? To highlight the drooping leaves of this amazing plant, I've placed it in a tall glazed ceramic pot and paired it with mistletoe cactus and spider plant, both of which will cascade over the edge. Purple waffle plants form shadows between the stromanthe and container, adding depth and contrast.

If you can't find the purple stromanthe used in this photo, there's a variegated one that's even more common and has patches of white, pink, and sage green that are sure to delight the kids. You could also use larger *Calathea* or *Maranta* species and get the same leaf-folding action, or use a Persian shield plant (*Strobilanthes*). For a few months after planting, you'll have to water enough to keep the top layer of soil moist, but once the plants get their long roots settled in, you can take those week-long vacations without worry. If the tips of the stromanthe's leaves begin to dry out, provide more humidity following the instructions on page 18. Feed these plants with a balanced houseplant fertilizer according to label instructions.

A B C D D

Orchid Shower Caddy

LIGHT	MOISTURE	HUMIDITY
Bright to sunny	Epiphytic	Average to high

Shopping List

- Wide bamboo container (or slat wood basket)
- Orchid bark
- (A) 1 butterfly orchid
  (*Epilaeliocattleya* 'Butterfly Kisses')
- (B) 1 soft cane orchid (*Dendrobium parishii*)
- (C) 1 moth orchid (*Phalaenopsis* spp.)
- (D) 4 string of coins (*Dischidia nummularia*)
- (E) 2 mistletoe cactus (*Rhipsalis baccifera*)

Plant Options

The beauty of this grouping is that almost any epiphyte will work. For best results, though, choose those that stay small and won't overtake their neighbors. Small Vriesea *and* Guzmania *hybrids are readily available at both garden centers and retailers, and dwarf moth orchids are also gaining popularity.*

The best place to grow humidity lovers is the bathroom, but who has room for plants with so many half-empty shampoo bottles and loofahs lying around? My solution is the orchid shower caddy: a hollowed-out bamboo segment that has been planted with orchids, bromeliads, and other epiphytes. The wire hanger allows you to hang it up at eye (and nose) level where it will perfume your shower and make you feel like you're in a steamy jungle waterfall. If your bathroom is too dark for plants, just keep it in a brighter room during the day and bring it with you to the bathtub. The luxurious vibe is totally worth the effort, especially when coupled with a romantic setting of bubbles, wine, and candlelight—and don't forget the music! This arrangement is greatly enhanced with the inclusion of fragrant orchids such as the *Dendrobium,* which can perfume your bathroom with their sweet fragrances. Just give orchids the "sniff test" before buying to make sure they actually have a scent.

Make your own bamboo orchid caddy by cutting a segment of thick-walled bamboo and making an opening with a jigsaw, or you can purchase one from one of the suppliers listed on page 170. If that seems like too much trouble, use anything from a slat wood orchid basket to a wire shower caddy. An hour before removing the orchids from their pots, soak the roots so that they become flexible and won't break in transit. Place the orchids' rootballs in the container, and then add divisions and cuttings of the mistletoe cactus, bromeliads, and string of coins to the spaces between the orchids. Once everything is in its place, slowly add orchid mix to the container and water them well to get them established. The cuttings will flourish in about a month as they start putting out new roots. Let the orchid mix dry at least a little between watering, and if placed in a bathroom, avoid getting soap or other products on the plants.

Out on a Limb

LIGHT	MOISTURE	HUMIDITY
Bright to sunny	Epiphytic	Average to high

Shopping List

- A slab of tree fern trunk
- Orchid bark
- **(A)** 1 bromeliad (*Vriesea sucrei* hybrid)
- **(B)** 1 mistletoe cactus (*Rhipsalis micrantha*)
- **(C)** 1 coral mistletoe cactus (*Rhipsalis cereuscula*)
- **(D)** 1 Easter cactus (*Hatiora gaertneri*)
- **(E)** 1 bird's nest fern (*Asplenium japonicum*)

Plant Options

One of my favorite things about epiphytes is that they're pretty foolproof. Almost any epiphytic orchid, fern, bromeliad, or cactus will work for this recipe, but I recommend using a bromeliad to serve as the focal point so that it doesn't look like a free-for-all. If Easter cactus and mistletoe cactus are unavailable, holiday cactus works well too.

Four years ago I mounted a bunch of epiphytes to a bowl-shaped slab of tree fern trunk and have since only given it only the bare minimum of water and fertilizer. I've even gone as long as a month without watering it! The Easter cactus has been blooming every year despite my shameful neglect, and even now after several weeks without water, red flower buds are forming at the ends of the shriveled and woody pads. The bromeliad and its progeny have bloomed twice since they were planted, each one putting out an impressive bright red feather containing multiple yellow flowers. Suffice to say, this is one very easy container recipe. The only recent addition is the bird's nest fern, but as it is also a durable epiphyte, it will thrive happily in its new home.

Planting the slab with epiphytes is incredibly easy. Purchase a slab of tree fern trunk or cork from your garden center or one of the vendors on page 170 and soak it in water before adding plants. If there isn't already a hole in the middle, carve out a depression in the slab with a sharp knife. Plant the fern in the pocket and fill in the gaps around the rootball with orchid mix or bark. The other plants can be affixed easily by tying them to the slab with wire or a twisty tie. Water thoroughly until each plant has grown roots and has become established. To keep the plants healthy and lush, feed periodically with a foliar spray such as compost tea, following the instructions on page 36. After blooming, the bromeliad will send out offsets that can be thinned out and separated by twisting and pulling away where the offset meets the parent plant. Display the slab on a dish, tile, or stone slab where excess water won't cause any damage to the furniture. Water the entire planting with a tank mister or spray bottle once a week, or by occasionally placing it in the sink under running water.

Pot of Plants at the End of the Rainbow

LIGHT	MOISTURE	HUMIDITY
Bright	Average to high	High

Shopping List

- Large container
- Regular potting mix
- **A** 2 Mamee crotons (*Codaieum* 'Mamee')
- **B** 3 Joseph's coat plants (*Alternanthera dentata* 'Little Ruby')
- **C** 3 maidenhair ferns (*Adiantum raddianum*)
- **D** 3 wax begonias (*Begonia semperflorens* cv.)

Plant Options

Because you aren't likely to find cobalt blue houseplants, start with a blue pot. Then find purple plants and green plants for the sides. It's a bit tricky to find plants with orange and yellow leaves like those of this croton, but coleus or a yellow-flowered lollipop plant make for good substitutes.

Kermit the frog would have flipped for this colorful container combo. I mean, I can actually picture him getting so excited about this rainbow connection that he would throw his limp, green-felted arms in the air wildly to celebrate. Remember long ago when Kermit asked "what's on the other side" of rainbows? Well, this is the answer. Always the philosophical amphibian, I'm pretty sure that he would enjoy the irony of finding not a pot of gold at the rainbow's end, but rather a pot of even more rainbow. What could be better than a rainbow that never goes away? To capture this supposed illusion, I started with a croton because it fades from nearly black to red, orange, and yellow. The purple Joseph's coat made the transition from blue to red, and the green maidenhair ferns filled the gap between blue and yellow. Small wax begonias were planted throughout to fill out the container and can be removed once the other plants fill in.

A mythical container combo such as this would vanish into thin air if the conditions weren't right, though. Much like real rainbows, the croton, Joseph's coat, ferns, and begonias in this planting have a thing for humidity and show their true beauty when the air is filled with tiny particles of water. Provide these magical conditions by keeping it in a humid well-lit bathroom, or mist it daily and take it to a shady spot outdoors in summer. The maidenhair fern is the most finicky of the group and will faint if the soil is allowed to dry out. Amend soil with coir to prevent this. As the plants fill in, thin branches and remove the plants that show the least vigor. Fertilize lightly with a diluted houseplant fertilizer monthly during the growing season.

Punchbowl Perfection

LIGHT	MOISTURE	HUMIDITY
Bright	Average	Average

Shopping List

- Large, wide container
- Regular potting mix
- **A** 2 chocolate soldier plants
  (*Episcia cupreata* 'Chocolate Soldier')
- **B** 1 peacock plant (*Calathea lancifolia*)
- **C** 2 lime pothos
  (*Epipremnum aureum* 'Neon')

Plant Options

*The only plant here that needs bright light and humidity is the chocolate soldier, but if you replace it with a more durable plant like a satin pothos, you'll get similar colors with less effort. The peacock plant can be replaced with a cast iron plant (*Aspidistra elatior*), rubber tree (*Ficus decora*), or any other fairly easy upright plant with dark leaves.*

You never forget your first container garden. While it wasn't my very first container recipe, this was the first one I made for this book, and it has been keeping me company in a corner of my studio ever since I started writing. Eventually the room filled up with other container gardens, but I still hold a soft spot for the one that started it all. The peacock plant seems to say "good night" every evening as it folds up its leaves and rustles against the shelves, and gently brushing the soft quilted foliage of the chocolate soldier has become a daily routine. The arrestingly bright lime green leaves of the pothos glow against the dark tones of the peacock plant and are even visible at night when I walk by for a glass of water. Even though pothos is the plant that stands out the most, it's the chocolate soldier that I happen to like the most. Every now and then it blooms in a show of fiery red flowers, adding even more excitement to the planting when I least expect it. When you make your own version of this recipe, you should know that the neon pothos is the secret ingredient that really makes it all work, but if you can't find one, use a *Philodendron hederaceum* 'Lemon-Lime' to get similarly chartreuse foliage on a vining plant.

Both the pothos and chocolate soldier will ramble over the edge of the bowl if allowed, so remove lanky stems as needed, or place longer stems of either on the surface of the soil where they will root and result in more vigorous plants. These plants can tolerate a fair amount of neglect, but keep the soil moist for the most consistent growth. Never allow the chocolate soldier to wilt as it will interrupt its lovely show of bright red flowers. Feed regularly with a houseplant fertilizer according to label instructions to get more blooms and healthier foliage.

Rainforest Drop

LIGHT	MOISTURE	HUMIDITY
Dim to sunny	Epiphytic	Average to high

Shopping List

- Grapevine ball
- Sphagnum moss
- **(A)** 2 crow's foot mistletoe cactus (*Rhipsalis micrantha*)
- **(B)** 1 pencil mistletoe cactus (*Rhipsalis baccifera*)
- **(C)** 4 coral mistletoe cacti (*Rhipsalis cereuscula*)
- **(D)** 1 air plant (*Tillandsia ionatha*)
- **(E)** 5 drunkard's dream plants (*Hatiora salicornioides*)

Plant Options

You'll be hard pressed to find plants as durable as mistletoe cacti, but Easter cacti (Hatiora gaertneri) *and holiday cacti* (Schlumbergera truncata) *are also pretty tough once established. If you have a sunny window, try using succulents.* Echeveria, Sedum, *and* Crassula *plants are all good choices as long as the sphagnum moss is allowed to dry out between waterings.*

Several years ago, I set out to reinvent the orchid pot. Not that there was necessarily anything wrong with orchid pots and slat wood baskets, but I was so captivated by the allure of the biodiversity of a rainforest branch that I just had to capture the scene on my own balcony. Many notes and sketches later, the idea came to me. I started stuffing a grapevine ball with sphagnum moss and mistletoe cactus cuttings and created the first of what I would eventually call rainforest drops: hanging orbs of lush rainforest life that could be grown in any home. I sold quite a few at first, but because they were so fun and easy to create, I decided that I would much rather just show people how to make their own. Use them at weddings as kissing balls and pomanders or hang one planted with mistletoe cactus over a doorway for some holiday romance.

This is a totally creative project, so the placement of each plant is really up to you. Stuff a grapevine ball with moistened sphagnum moss, insert epiphytic plants root-first, and tuck them in place with more moss. Planting unrooted cuttings will also work, but to get them established faster, just divide a container and plant them with roots intact. Orchids, succulents, peperomias, and bromeliads can all be planted in the same way. Display the rainforest drop by hanging it from the ceiling, mounting on the wall, or setting it atop a dish or tabletop. Water once every week by spraying with a tank mister or by removing the ball and holding it under running water in the sink. If you start to notice bald spots, just insert more plugs of cuttings to help it regain a full head of lushness. So that it doesn't look lopsided, make sure you plant the whole ball rather than just one side. Leave a small gap open so you can hang it from the ceiling or the wall!

Raspberry Margarita

LIGHT	MOISTURE	HUMIDITY
Bright to sunny	Low to average	Average

Shopping List

- Large container
- Regular potting mix
- Orchid mix
- **(A)** 4 queen's tears (*Billbergia hoelscheriana*)
- **(B)** 1 queen's tears (*Billbergia* 'White Cloud')
- **(C)** 1 earth star (*Cryptanthus bivittatis* 'Red Star')
- **(D)** 2 Vriesea bromeliads (*Vriesea vagans*)
- **(E)** 5 pseudorhipsalis plants
  (*Pseudorhipsalis ramulosa*)

Plant Options

Most Billbergia *bromeliads would make nice substitutes for the one in this planting, but silver vase plant (*Aechmea fasciata*) is another more common bromeliad to use. If you find it hard to find epiphytic cacti like the* Pseudorhipsalis *used here, try swapping it and the shorter bromeliads out for succulents, which will thrive along with the queen's tears in a sunny windowsill.*

It might be hard to believe, but the graceful queen's tears looking over this arrangement are nothing more than overlooked weeds here in Florida. They were shared between gardeners back in the days before home-improvement centers and were left to fend for themselves after the gardeners and their gardens faded into memory. Most *Billbergia* species in my collection were rescued from abandoned lots, where their tan leaves lay camouflaged against the dead grass as a subtle reminder that someone once had gardens there. Take these diamonds out of the rough, however, and they sparkle. When grown in bright or direct light, the leaves color and develop cream-colored dapples and spots like freckles in reverse; in lower light they revert back to arched leaves in a hue of olive green. I used a medium cream-colored container to tie in with the billbergia's spots and complemented its pink and green coloration with an earth star, more bromeliads, and a few pink *Pseudorhipsalis* cacti.

There are hundreds of *Billbergia* species, but the one that you're most likely to find is *Billbergia nutans*. It still has the dangling queen's tears flowers, but the narrow leaves are green and gracefully arching as opposed to the stiff and upright serrated leaves of *B. hoelscheriana*. A friend of mine dubbed it "knife plant" for the resemblance. Wear gloves when planting these, as some might experience a slight irritation from the sharp leaves. These epiphytes are very drought tolerant, so as long as you let water collect in the cups of the bromeliads, you can go a week or two without watering. Rinse them occasionally to prevent stagnant water from collecting and rotting the plant. Fertilizing isn't really necessary, but a diluted serving of orchid food or compost tea every several months will keep plants growing vigorously.

Ruby Red

LIGHT	MOISTURE	HUMIDITY
Bright	Average	Average

Shopping List

- Large container
- Regular potting mix
- **A** 1 red aglaonema (*Aglaonema* 'Siam Red')
- **B** 1 Cuban oregano
  (*Plectranthus amboinicus*)
- **C** 2 arrow vines (*Syngonium podophyllum*)
- **D** 1 pink episcia (*Episcia* 'Pink Heaven')

Plant Options

Because these plants have very basic requirements, there are many houseplants that will work in their stead. To get the pink leaves, though, you'll have to turn to caladiums, pink Neoregelia *bromeliads, or perhaps a* Dracaena marginata *'Colorama'. However you manage to find a pink-leaved plant, the effect is well worth the effort!*

Stuffed with rambunctious plants and ready to burst, this cocktail of tropical flavors has the fullness you might expect from a traditional flower-filled outdoor container combo. If the veined lime-green arrow vine doesn't take over the pot first, you can expect the fragrant Cuban oregano or pink episcia to jostle their way to dominance. The red aglaonema is a new plant on the scene with ruby red edges, but has proven to be every bit as durable as the ones to which you've become accustomed to seeing in waiting rooms. As the other plants mound and topple over, the red aglaonema will grow upward in a clump of exotic foliage that's unusual enough to warrant a second look. Sample the soft and pungent leaves of the Cuban oregano and incorporate it in meals, or just enjoy its spicy aroma on its own. The whole medley definitely looks good enough to eat, but do not—I repeat, *do not*—eat the other plants in the pot as they are all inedible, if not poisonous. Never eat a plant unless you know exactly what it is.

The downside to a bountiful and overstuffed group planting is that you will need to keep it well groomed. It's best to remove one of the two arrow vines once they've filled in so the other plants don't get smothered. Remove any long stems that reach the ground, and if desired, propagate them using the steps on page 37. Provide as much indirect light as possible so that the episcia can produce its deep reddish orange blooms. Keep the compost moist at all times to keep growth steady. Avoid letting moisture collect on the leaves of the episcia, as it will cause the hairy leaves to rot. Fertilize with a balanced houseplant fertilizer occasionally to keep those lush leaves coming, and repot the plants into a larger container if they become rootbound.

Satin and Sage

LIGHT	MOISTURE	HUMIDITY
Low to bright	Average	Average

Shopping List

- Large container
- Regular potting mix
- **(A)** 1 satin pothos
  (*Scindapsus pictus* 'Argyraeus')
- **(B)** 2 parlor palms
  (*Chamaedorea elegans*)
- **(C)** 2 dracaenas
  (*Dracaena deremensis* 'Lemon Lime')

Plant Options

These plants are all relatively easy to find, with the exception of the 'Argyraeus' satin pothos. I highly recommend seeking it out, but you can always substitute a 'Marble Queen' pothos or a chocolate soldier if needed, because they're both beautiful in their own right. The dracaena can be replaced by any other dracaena that's available.

It isn't very often that the "spiller" steals the limelight from the "thriller" but *Scindapsus pictus* 'Argyraeus' is one impressive vine. Satin pothos is a golden pothos relative with velvety sage green leaves so big and silvery that it easily becomes the focal point of the arrangement. Guests will find themselves stopping to feel the leathery leaves for themselves, which feel a lot like worn leather or suede compared to the glossier houseplants to which they might be familiar. Make sure you get the 'Argyraeus' cultivar, as the regular species has small dark green leaves and this one has big and silvery leaves that stand out in the dark. To take advantage of that light silver-colored foliage, I've placed it in front of a *Dracaena* 'Lemon Lime' and a planting of deep green parlor palms. Both the *Dracaena* and the parlor palms will grow upward to create an impressive screen, while the pothos will hang toward the ground. Place the planter on a raised surface such as a coffee table so that the vine has plenty of room to hang out. Even though the satin pothos is clearly the main event, keep an eye out for those tropical-looking parlor palms in the back, as they'll eventually get so tall and lush that they'll impart a definitive island feel to your room.

Each of these plants is durable and will be able to handle a week without water in a pinch. This is one of the few combos in this book that can handle a dimly lit room, but a brighter location will give the dracaena a denser, more attractive form. Parlor palms are usually sold as pots filled with seedlings so that they look fuller, and it's very likely that at least some of the seedlings will die in the shadows of the others. Remove any dead leaves or stems to let more light reach the other palms and to minimize pests.

Shades of Gray

LIGHT	MOISTURE	HUMIDITY
Sunny	Low	Low

Shopping List

- Medium container
- Cactus potting mix
- **(A)** 1 silver teaspoons plant (*Kalanchoe bracteata*)
- **(B)** 3 string of pearls (*Senecio rowleyanus*)
- **(C)** 2 wandering Jew plants (*Tradescantia zebrina*)
- **(D)** 3 echeverias (*Echeveria glauca*)
- **(E)** 1 black earth star (*Cryptanthus zonatus*)

Plant Options

It isn't too hard to find succulents with gray leaves, but some worthwhile ones to use around the edges of the pot include ghost plant (Graptopetalum paraguayense), *Echeveria glauca, and Echeveria 'Topsy Turvy'. For the large plant in the center, use panda plant* (Kalanchoe tomentosa) *or a spiny Madagascar palm* (Pachypodium lamerei) *for height.*

I started to read the critically acclaimed book *50 Shades of Grey* with breathless trepidation and anticipated an exciting foray into a tantalizing topic that delights me to no end. So you can imagine my disappointment when I came to realize not only was the book not about the scandalous subject of color theory, but it hadn't the slightest thing to do with gray at all! Since author E. L. James failed to deliver the love letter to achromatic (without color) color schemes that I had been expecting, I suppose that it's up to me to share my passion for a hue that, while appreciated in photography and film, is sadly overlooked in the garden. A gray plant is actually pretty special. Gray plants like the *Echeveria* and *Kalanchoe* in this arrangement only *appear* to be gray. They only look that way because of the dense arrangement of tiny hairs that reflect the light and prevent moisture loss. It works in our favor for this design, as each plant exudes a sense of timelessness and sophistication, and the wood-stamped concrete planter only serves to solidify the impression. To add a little bit of depth and interest to an otherwise boring design, I've included a black earth star and a groundcover of purple-black wandering Jew.

Put these voyeurs on full display in a sunny window and rotate the container periodically so that each plant can be exposed to the sun's harsh rays. If the wandering Jew becomes overgrown, remove the longest stems at its base. Mealybugs sometimes appear on the silver teaspoons but can be easily removed by hand. The earth star requires some humidity to thrive, so swap it out with another black plant like *Echeveria* 'Black Prince' if humidity needs cannot be met. Otherwise, these plants take punishment so well that they almost seem to enjoy it, so there's no need to pamper them with too much water.

Shady Succulence

LIGHT	MOISTURE	HUMIDITY
Bright to sunny	Low	Low

Shopping List

- Large container
- Cactus potting mix
- **(A)** 1 snake plant
  (*Sansevieria* 'Bantel's Sensation')
- **(B)** 3 window-leaved haworthia plants
  (*Haworthia marumiana* cv. *batesiana*)

Plant Options

Any Haworthia *or* Gasteria *plants would do well at the base of the snake plant, but for a more shade-tolerant recipe, replace them with bird's nest snake plants (*Sansevieria hahnii*). If Sansevieria 'Bantel's Sensation' proves elusive, there's no need to worry. Any snake plant will do. The most common one has wider leaves and golden edges.*

No houseplants are better suited to living tapestries than succulents, but unfortunately most of them require direct sun to be at their best. Since I began my obsession with gardening, I've been inspired by the creative works of living art created by gardeners out west and wanted to start making rich tapestries of succulents in my own apartment. But with only a small south-facing window to provide direct sunlight, it would have appeared that I was out of luck—that is, until I learned about the shadier side of succulents. This arrangement captures the best of both worlds and is small enough to fit anywhere, yet tall enough to make an impact. The most popular of the shade-tolerant succulents is the snake plant, and for good reason! Going above and beyond the standard-issue variegated snake plant, I used the dramatic and unusual *Sansevieria* hybrid 'Bantel's Sensation' to form the centerpiece. The surrounding groundcover of window-leaved haworthia echoes the colors of the snake plant and forms a subtle contrast against the dark brown container, appearing almost like a bed of moss at the foot of the snake plant.

This arrangement looks a lot more natural if the plants are separated and replanted. Plant the snake plant centerpiece as a 4-inch container, or divide a larger planting using the directions on page 38. To keep each of the divisions from falling over while planting, wrap twine around the leaves until the planting is complete. Make the dense groundcover of *Haworthia* by gently pulling apart the rosettes in each container and place them on the soil surface so that they sit just below the lip of the pot. Because it's hard to tuck soil in between the tightly packed plants, use a funnel to pour sand or vermiculite between each plant. From spring through fall, let the soil dry out between watering, and water sparingly in winter.

Small World

LIGHT	MOISTURE	HUMIDITY
Bright	Average	Average

Shopping List

- ■ Extra-large shallow container
- ■ Regular potting mix
- ■ Gravel
- ■ Flat stones or pottery shards
- ■ **A** 1 weeping fig (*Ficus benjamina* 'Variegata')
- ■ **B** 3 foxtail ferns (*Asparagus densiflorus*)
- ■ **C** 2 Scotch moss plants (*Sagina subulata*)
- ■ **D** 1 English ivy (*Hedera helix* cvv.)
- ■ **E** 1 mondo grass (*Ophiopogon japonicus* 'Nana')

Plant Options

*Miniature houseplants are hard to find, so rather than get too specific, I'll just tell you what to look for: slow growth and small leaves. Spikemosses (*Selaginella *spp.) and small ferns are great for their fine foliage, as are peperomias with small leaves. The weeping fig is common enough but can be replaced with any other tree-form houseplant. Ming aralia is a good one.*

With scissors and spoons replacing lawnmowers and shovels, tending to this tiny garden feels a lot like the real thing but without any of the backache. Miniature gardens recreate a realistic scene using small plants, but this one has a few tricks up its sleeve to make it seem even more life-like. Oh, and this little garden is actually quite large too. Planted in the largest bonsai pot I could find, with a sizable weeping fig, it demands a large counter or tabletop to be displayed to the best effect. To make the diorama even more lifelike, I used a little trick called forced perspective. This was accomplished by placing plants with larger leaves in the foreground and, those with smaller leaves in the background. Foxtail ferns form what appear to be tiny pine trees on a hillside in the distance, along with "shrubs" of clumps of decorative lichen. Black sand makes the background appear to recede while lighter-toned gravel and stones in the foreground seem to jump forward, making the lush groundcover of dwarf mondo grass and ivy appear larger than life.

The only tricky part to planting this miniature garden is getting the weeping fig's rootball to fit in the shallow pot. Gently tease apart the lower portion of the rootball so that the crown of the tree is level with the lip of the container. Fan the roots out along the bottom of the container so they can establish. Use a nozzle to wash away the top layer of soil, exposing the roots. Prune the lower limbs to minimize transplant shock and impart a pleasing tree-like shape. Next add the other plants, forming hills and valleys in the soil as you go. Finish the garden with decorative mulches such as stones, gravel, and bark. Keep soil moist and prune as needed . . . or desired. You'll have so much fun that you'll plant ryegrass seeds just so you can have an excuse to mow the lawn!

Solar Eclipse

LIGHT	MOISTURE	HUMIDITY
Sunny	Low to average	Low

Shopping List

- Small, wide container
- Cactus potting mix
- **A** 4 haworthia plants (*Haworthia* spp.)
- **B** 3 gold dot sedums (*Sedum* 'Gold Dot')
- **C** 1 haworthia plant (*Haworthia coarctata*)
- **D** 1 peperomia (*Peperomia*)
- **E** 1 cremnosedum plant (*Cremnosedum* 'Little Gem')
- **F** 1 bromeliad plant (*Neoregelia* 'Wild Tiger')

Plant Options

You'll be hard pressed to find another plant like Peperomia graveolens, *but it's worth looking into another window leaf peperomia such as 'Peppy' or* Peperomia dolabriformis. *The sedums require more water than the others in the group, but larger ones like burro's tail (*Sedum morganianum*) and jelly bean plant (*Sedum rubrotinctum*) will handle drier conditions.*

It starts with a pretty flowerpot, and the next thing you know, your shopping cart is full and your wallet is empty. Sure, your creativity can get expensive sometimes, but it's usually worth it. When I saw this bright candy-apple-red pot at the garden center, I just had to find some plants to justify my impulsive purchase, but after about fifteen minutes of fruitless searching, I returned the pot to its shelf and applauded myself for saving twenty bucks. But then I noticed it right there in line at the checkout: a plant that seemed tailor-made to complement the red pot and would likely be sold to someone else if I didn't act fast. It was *Peperomia graveolens*, and it had—get this—glossy red succulent leaves with clear "windows" on their surfaces, much like a red sports car with a sunroof. I didn't need a sports car, but I could certainly justify buying a plant that looked like one. Combined with nearly black haworthias and bright gold dot sedums, the peperomia stands out even more and actually seems to be an extension of the planter itself. Display this arrangement in an eclectically decorated room or use it to add excitement to parties and barbecues by bringing it outside to a table on the patio during summer.

As it turns out, the *Peperomia graveolens* is also a really easy plant and has done well in both direct sun and bright indirect light. However, grow them in a south-facing window for the best appearance. Allow the soil's top inch to dry out between watering, but don't let it dry out completely or the gold dot sedums will start to lose their lower leaves. To keep the sedums from getting leggy, keep them facing the window for the most light. If the haworthias fill the pot and become rootbound, follow the steps on page 38 to divide and repot.

Spa Treatment

LIGHT	MOISTURE	HUMIDITY
Sunny	Average	Average

Shopping List

- Medium container
- Regular potting mix
- **A** 1 lady palm (*Rhapis excelsa*)
- **B** 1 painted fingernail plant
  (*Neoregelia spectablis*)
- **C** 2 firecracker plants
  (*Russelia equisetiformis*)

Plant Options

If you find yourself doing a double take upon seeing the lady palm's price tag, choose another shade-tolerant one like the parlor palm (Chamaedorea elegans) or the kentia palm (Howea forsteriana). Firecracker plant isn't as common as it should be, so if you need a replacement try using ferns or spider plant. Any bromeliad will work well in place of the painted fingernail plant.

Spas are selling some pretty freaky treatments nowadays. For the right price you can have your stinky feet nibbled upon by tiny fish with a taste for psoriasis, or if so inclined, you and a loved one can share a bath filled with blood-red wine. If these sound more like scenes from horror movies to you, maybe a peaceful Asian-themed container planting would be enough to relieve your anxiety. It has all of the perks of a water feature but without the headache! To make the whole grouping look cohesive and focused, start out with a substantial earthenware pot and choose plants with a minimalist aesthetic. Lady palm combines the best features of palms with those of bamboos with narrow upright stems and delicately fingered fans of glossy green foliage, while the firecracker plant cascades over the edge of the pot in a shower of tubular red flowers. I've included a painted fingernail plant to serve as the focal point, but any plant with a fountain-like form, such as bird's nest fern, dracaena, or spider plant, will do. Place this planter near the shower or a favorite reading spot, and your worries will feel worlds away.

The bromeliad in the photo is colorful because it was grown in a sunny spot, but will revert to a glossy olive green if grown in bright light. Add a mulch of orchid bark for a naturalistic look and to simulate dark-stained teak and mahogany. Caring for these plants is relatively simple but be prepared to occasionally remove the firecracker plants' longest stems to keep them in scale. Spent blooms also fall to the ground, so place the planter on a solid surface such as tile or wood to make cleanup easier. If all of this sounds a bit too messy for your taste, replace the firecracker plant with mistletoe cactus or a trailing *Peperomia* or *Hoya* and add more orchid bark to the top layer. Feed with either a houseplant fertilizer or one formulated especially for palms.

Storm Clouds at Sunset

LIGHT	MOISTURE	HUMIDITY
Sunny	Low	Low to average

Shopping List

- Large container
- Cactus potting mix
- **(A)** 1 earth star (*Cryptanthus* 'Pink Starlight')
- **(B)** 3 ghost plants (×*Graptopetalum paraguayense*)
- **(C)** 3 graptosedum plants (×*Graptosedum* 'Bronze')
- **(D)** 2 stonecrop plants (*Sedum spurium* 'Red Carpet')

Plant Options

Replace the large earth star with another bromeliad or a large succulent such as an aloe or agave. The trick to planting any container groupings with behemoths like these is to use plants with stems that spread out beneath the expanding leaves, and won't get smothered. Good bets include sedums and echeverias.

One of the most exhilarating experiences in gardening is growing something that none of the other kids on your street have, and this enormous earth star is one such plant. Will you be able to easily find a *Cryptanthus* for yourself at your local garden center? Maybe not, but don't let that keep you from finding your own special plant as a substitute. Between all of the bromeliads and succulents available out there both in stores and online (page 170), you're sure to find one that's just as unique as my own earth star specimen. Regardless of what plant you use as the centerpiece in the design, the basic formula for this planting is to use a large succulent or bromeliad and underplant it with succulents that will stand out between the main plant and the container. The goal is to showcase your special centerpiece, so use a container that stands in stark contrast to the color of the plant. White and black usually work quite well. Display your trophy in front of a window so that all of the neighbors can stop and stare in utter disbelief at your good fortune. You can always share divisions with them if you're feeling particularly charitable, following the steps on page 38.

When planting the succulents, it helps to bend back some of the earth star's lower leaves so that you have room to nestle in the succulents by their rootballs. Don't be afraid to prune out the more stubborn leaves to make room either. To make watering a bit easier, use a watering can or tank mister with a narrow spout and tuck it under the leaves at the edge of the container. This ensures that water makes to the root zone rather than the carpet. After blooming, the *Cryptanthus* will form offsets in the center of the plant. Leave these in place or remove a couple to pot up on their own.

A Tempting Terrarium

LIGHT	MOISTURE	HUMIDITY
Bright	Average	Low (moisture is contained inside)

Shopping List

- Terrarium
- Regular potting mix
- Activated charcoal
- Decorative rocks
- **A** 1 spikemoss (*Selaginella flabellate*)
- **B** 1 rabbit's foot fern (*Davallia canariensis*)
- **C** 1 anthurium (*Anthurium scherzerianum*)
- **D** 4 earth stars
  (*Cryptanthus bromelioides tricolor*)
- **E** 1 peperomia (*Peperomia* 'Bianco Verde')

Plant Options

Planting a terrarium is great because you can use some of the humidity-loving plants that you wouldn't be able to grow elsewhere in the home. Most spikemosses (Selaginella spp.) are good choices, as are African violets, nerve plants (Fittonia cv.), and small begonias. If you decide to include bromeliads or orchids, elevate them on driftwood or bark so that they don't rot in the moist soil.

The world would be a very different place were it not for the rather accidental invention of the terrarium. Around 1829, Dr. Nathaniel Bagshaw Ward looked inside a glass jar holding one of his butterfly cocoons and noticed that a tiny fern and grass plant had sprouted in the sealed container, surviving on nothing more than the humid air behind the glass. His discovery meant that orchids and other exotic plants could be transported overseas and grown indoors by British gardeners. Remember now, they had no central heating to keep tropical plants warm and also had to deal with pollution that made growing behind glass a necessity. We might be blessed with cleaner and warmer air now, but I think you'll agree that terrariums have yet to lose their appeal. This one uses a variety of plants well suited for a life under glass and will give you a nice view in the morning if placed on a dresser or a desk.

To plant the terrarium, first remove the glass panes for better access. Then add a shallow layer of gravel for drainage. Arrange larger plants on the surface of the gravel as desired, teasing apart the roots to lay flat along the soil. Add more soil to cover the roots and then nestle earth stars into the soil. Add dimension and interest by adding features like hills and streams. To make the hill, create a mound around a rootball with coir and place small plants on the face of the mound. To make a streambed of river rocks, simply lay them on top of the drainage layer and keep the rocks free of growth and debris as the plants begin to grow. After planting, only water the terrarium once the compost has begun to dry out. If the terrarium starts to smell sour, remove dead leaves, inspect for pests, and let it air out before resuming normal care.

Thumbelina

LIGHT	MOISTURE	HUMIDITY
Sunny	Low	Low

Shopping List

- Extra-small container
- Cactus potting mix
- **(A)** 2 living stone plants (*Lithops* spp.)
- **(B)** 3 divisions of haworthia (*Haworthia* spp.)
- **(C)** 2 cuttings of jelly bean plant (*Sedum rubrotinctum* 'Mini')

Plant Options

You don't need the haworthia and jelly bean plant for this tiny garden, and most succulents will work well if you take cuttings and treat the display as something in between a cut flower arrangement and a container garden. When the cuttings root and get too large, replace them with new ones. If living stones seem like too much trouble, replace them with real stones.

You don't need a big glazed ceramic pot to make an indoor container garden with big impact, and coming in at less than 3 inches wide, this featherweight packs quite a punch. How many different kinds of plants do you see in that tiny container? If you saw the tiny pine trees and shrubs imitated by *Haworthia* and *Sedum* and answered "two," look closely at the oddly symmetrical pebbles in the sand. Those living stones are really plants! I know what you're thinking. "Where will I find plants this small?" You'll notice I specified you use two *cuttings* of the jelly bean plant and three *Haworthia* divisions, because you'll be hard pressed to find too many plants sold in centimeter-wide containers. You can substitute the sedum cuttings with those of any other small-leaved succulent, but don't expect them to be anything more than temporary additions. Because the living stone requires total dryness half of the year, the cuttings will have to be swapped out as they wither away. Before planting the haworthia, gently tease apart the offsets. Then arrange the divisions as desired along with the living stones in cactus mix and top with a shallow layer of decorative sand.

Living stones have very specific requirements but are nonetheless nearly maintenance-free. Water following this schedule: In summer, water only if the leaves begin to shrivel. In fall, (starting in August) water deeply to initiate growth, allowing the soil to completely dry between watering. In winter, do not water at all. If the haworthia becomes shriveled, remove it to be watered separately and replace. By spring the leaves will have been reduced to papery husks, at which point you can begin watering again as you did in fall. New growth will push out of the dead leaves and start anew. Don't be discouraged if they shrivel up, though, as they are some of the more difficult plants in the book. Real, non-living stones are a lot more forgiving.

Tinsel of Tillandsia

LIGHT	MOISTURE	HUMIDITY
Bright	Average	Average

Shopping List

- Extra-small container
- Regular potting mix
- Orchid mix
- **A** 1 holiday cactus
  (*Schlumbergera × buckleyi*)
- **B** 5 air plants (*Tillandsia ionatha*)

Plant Options

Just about any Tillandsia *species will work well for this combination, so choose whichever ones are available at the nursery. Anthuriums, nerve plants, and orchids are other good choices for the centerpiece, and they can be swapped out throughout the year with houseplants that have shorter displays, such as bulbs, mums, and Philippine violets.*

It seems like holiday houseplants always lose their cheer by the time the Christmas tree makes it to the curb. Poinsettias get straggly, amaryllis bulbs become boring, and Norfolk Island pines just get too big for their britches. But a Christmas cactus with all the trimmings of *Tillandsia* will keep its magic long after its flowers fade away—and if you use an assortment of different air plants, you'll be treated to bonus blooms throughout the year. You can use any "holiday" cactus regardless of the holiday, and Easter cactus, Mother's Day cactus, and Thanksgiving cactus are all fair game. Holiday cacti form berries after blooming and continue to keep their attractive leaf-like stems throughout the year, but if you need a makeshift centerpiece, just swap it out with the plant of your choice and place the air plants back over the new plant's container.

Here's what makes this holiday arrangement so versatile: the *Tillandsia* plants and holiday cactus are entirely removable. Using gravel or a free-draining medium, fill the container up until there's about 5 inches of space from the surface to the top of the pot. Then set the 4-inch container of holiday cactus on the gravel layer so the container's lip rests right below that of the surrounding pot. Fill the remaining space in the pot with decorative mulch, leaving about half an inch of space above, and arrange the air plants on the surface so that they comfortably sit in place. Water the cactus and air plants with a tank sprayer or mister every few days, and replace the cactus as needed. To keep the holiday cactus blooming every year, bring it outdoors or to a cool spot in fall so that the cool temperatures will encourage it to form flower buds. If it is taken outdoors, protect from frost. If you tend to overwater your holiday cactus, another option is to grow the holiday cactus in orchid mix or bark to mimic its natural habitat.

Tropical Canopy

LIGHT	MOISTURE	HUMIDITY
Bright	Average	Average

Shopping List

- Extra-large container
- Regular potting mix
- Orchid bark (optional)
- (A) 1 fiddle leaf fig (*Ficus lyrata*)
- (B) 1 flaming feather bromeliad (*Vriesea carinata*)
- (C) 2 comet bromeliads (*Vriesea* 'Komet')
- (D) 3 trailing peperomias (*Peperomia* 'Isabella')
- (E) 4 ZZ plants (*Zamioculcas zamifolia*)

Plant Options

Use any Ficus *or* Schefflera *to replace the fiddle leaf fig. Grow any assortment of bromeliads, orchids, or other epiphytes at the base of the tree, but be sure to include another trailing plant if* Peperomia *'Isabella' is unavailable. Wax vines (*Hoya *spp.), mistletoe cacti (*Rhipsalis *spp.), and* Dischidia *plants are good choices, but philodendrons or pothos will work in a pinch.*

It takes a tree to raise a village, and the aggressive roots of a *Ficus* tree can do just that. In the tropics they lift sidewalks, roads, and building foundations and have even been known to "strangle" houses with their hanging aerial roots. Most houseplants won't last for long when planted alongside those choking and aggressive roots, but a handful of special plants can actually co-exist peacefully with a foe such as a ficus. Because their roots fill the pot and quickly drink up moisture, the solution is to use plants that already cope with these very same conditions in the treetops of the rainforest: epiphytes. Since *Vriesea* bromeliads can absorb water and nutrients using nothing more than their cupped leaves, they can be planted right over the soilless rootball of the *Ficus*. A planting of chartreuse *Peperomia* 'Isabella' will drape over the pot's edge and spread as a fine-textured groundcover. ZZ plants take root competition and deep shade in stride and create a deep emerald-green backdrop of tall leathery leaves. Place this grouping on the floor so that the ficus has plenty of room to tower overhead and transform your home into wild jungle.

They can survive a couple weeks without water once established, but keep the soil evenly moist for the best growth. Water each plant including the mounted *Tillandsia* plants and bromeliads, so that everything gets enough moisture. Thin overgrown plants by division, and prune the lower stems of the *Ficus* so that more light reaches the plants below. If the tree becomes too large for the container, repot the whole grouping or cut the tallest stems to the ground. They will re-sprout where they've been cut. To fertilize, spray the entire planting (leaves and all) with a spray bottle or tank mister of water-soluble fertilizer or compost tea diluted according to label instructions.

Vertically Verdant

LIGHT	MOISTURE	HUMIDITY
Bright	Average	Average

Shopping List

- Wall planter (GroVert™)
- Regular potting mix
- **A** 2 chocolate soldiers (*Episcia* 'Chocolate Soldier)
- **B** 3 lipstick plants (*Aeschynanthus radicans*)
- **C** 2 peperomia plants (*Peperomia scanders*)
- **D** 1 button fern (*Pellaea rotundifolia*)
- **E** 1 peperomia (*Peperomia glabella*)
- **F** 1 neon pothos (*Epipremnum aureum* 'Neon')

Plant Options

You can use all sorts of different plants to get this look, but avoid planting anything that gets too big or has aggressive root systems. If you plant a trunked houseplant like a Dracaena, *keep in mind that the stem will eventually start to grow upward and result in a different look than planned.*

Imagine a painting that literally comes to life, reaching beyond the frame with rambling leaves and exotic blooms. There are lots of options for growing your own living wall, from DIY projects to readymade kits, but the wrong choice could end in soggy carpets and walls. This sturdy framed GroVert planter from Bright Green is ideal because it has a built-in watering system that keeps your plants' roots moist and your walls dry. You can purchase the planter unit by itself or add a wooden frame (pictured) that can be stained or painted to match your décor. Most houseplants will thrive when grown vertically, but I chose vines that will lay flat against the wall and can be easily pruned as needed. Lipstick vine produces beautiful red flowers that push out of their burgundy lipstick cases, and the velvet-textured chocolate soldier puts on a show with similarly bright red blooms. Even when the other plants aren't blooming, the bright lime green leaves of neon pothos provide a striking contrast against the deep brown-stained frame.

Planting and hanging the vertical garden is easier than you'd think. First, remove the plastic planter from the frame and set it aside. Stain or paint the frame, allowing it to dry. Returning to the plastic planter, place moisture mats in each opening and place it inside the frame. Insert plants, packing potting mix around the roots it in tightly. Water well after planting and lay flat for up to two weeks before hanging so that the roots have time to establish and secure the loose soil. Once the roots have had time to spread out, hang the wood frame using the supplied mounting. Watering is very simple: just fill the irrigator with water and let it percolate through the moisture mats.

Victorian Vavoom

LIGHT	MOISTURE	HUMIDITY
Low to bright	Average	Average

Shopping List

- Medium container
- Regular potting mix
- **A** 1 cast iron plant (*Aspidistra* 'Milky Way')
- **B** 2 variegated English ivies (*Hedera helix*)
- **C** 1 ruffled fern
  (*Nephrolepsis* 'Fluffy Ruffles')
- **D** 2 strawberry begonia plants
  (*Saxifraga stolonifera*)

Plant Options

Cast iron plants, ivies, and ferns are so very Victorian, so try to use them if you can. They're all relatively easy to find, but if you still need a replacement, try using creeping fig (Ficus pumila) to replace the ivy and Chinese evergreen (Aglaonema spp.) to replace the cast iron plant.

Victorian England was an exciting time for indoor plants. As the smoggy cities of England filled to their brims and technology became more advanced, city dwellers anxiously followed the adventures of so-called plant hunters in exotic lands abroad and tried to replicate the distant jungles with houseplants in their own homes. Glass conservatories housed the most exhilarating selection of tropical specimens by collecting the heat of the sun and holding in moist air, but the average homeowner had to make do with crude heating and low light levels. Displayed in a rustic weathered terracotta azalea pot, this container combination is similar to one you would see in a Victorian conservatory. The cast iron plant at the center of the arrangement was favored for its steely resolve and durability in dark and drafty situations, while the English ivy along the edge was popular for tolerating the cold temperatures of unheated homes and giving the impression of the familiar views that could be found outdoors. The ruffled fern both exemplifies the tastes of the Victorian age and imparts a soft and tactile appeal that smooths over the harsh lines of the cast iron plant.

Cast iron plant is as tough as iron nails, but the fern and ivy need humidity to thrive. Provide humidity using the methods on page 18, or do it the old-fashioned way—with a cloche. Also known as a bell jar, cloches are glass domes that were placed over plants to protect them from the elements. But today they're used mostly for their decorative appeal. Ivies also like it cool in winter, so move the planter to an unheated area if it starts to suffer. If kept happy, each of the plants will proceed to spread throughout the container with utter abandon, so take divisions once every two years and prune the ivy as needed. For the best growth, feed with a general houseplant fertilizer according to label instruction.

Windowsill Herb Garden

LIGHT	MOISTURE	HUMIDITY
Sunny	Average	Average

Shopping List

- Small container
- Regular potting mix
- **(A)** 2 oregano plants (*Oreganum vulgare*)
- **(B)** 1 variegated basil plant
  (*Ocimum × citriodorum*)

Plant Options

Most herbs will work well in this combo. Other suitable herbs include thyme, salvia, oregano, chives, or mint. If you do choose to grow mint, double-pot the invasive herb so that it doesn't smother the others in the planting. If you prefer, plant smaller herbs in the gaps while you wait for the three big ones to fill out.

Herbs really are a chef's best friend. A simple planting of tasty herbs in a window box is just the right size for a sunny kitchen windowsill, and you'll be able to pluck off snippets and sprigs whenever you choose. You can even bring them to a dimly lit dining room for the evening so that family and guests can pick their own herbs to garnish and flavor their supper. When it comes to the herbs you choose for your own windowsill garden, you're only limited by the space on your windowsill, but the most effective arrangements include multiples of one herb to visually unify the scene. I chose an oregano for its dense habit, and because it provides a pungent pick-me-up to tomato dishes, particularly Italian ones. The centerpiece, however, is the variegated basil. Its brightly variegated leaves seem to glow against the finer foliage of the oregano, and it could easily be grown for its appearance alone. The grouping might look sparse when newly planted, but be patient. They'll get bushy in no time!

These fair-weather friends will get cranky if they don't get enough light, so place them in a windowsill where they'll get at least four hours of direct sun each day. They will lean toward the light, so turn the container around periodically to keep it looking full and balanced. Sometimes pests such as mealybugs and spidermites will appear, but they are easily removed by knocking them loose with a spray of water in the kitchen sink. Severe infestations can be treated by mixing one teaspoon of dish soap to a gallon of water and spraying the foliage. Keep the soil moist at all times, and fertilize regularly according to label instructions to keep them cranking out those yummy leaves. Just don't expect them to last for too long, because even with the best possible care, you're likely to see your tasty friends bite the dust. That is, if you don't end up biting them first.

RESOURCES

ONLINE RETAIL NURSERIES

- www.tropiflora.com
- www.store.brentandbeckysbulbs.com
- www.glasshouseworks.com
- www.logees.com
- www.stokestropicals.com
- www.stevesleaves.com
- www.thesucculentgarden.com
- www.almostedenplants.com

WHOLESALE NURSERIES

- www.excelsagardens.com
- www.ngmpro.com
- www.cfferns.com

MATERIALS

- Pruners—www.fiskars.com
- Trowels—www.gardentoolcompany.com

- Artificial Lighting—www.sunlightsupply.com
- Potting Mix—www.sungro.com
- Vertical Gardens—www.brightgreenusa.com
- Plant Stands—www.ezmountplantpothanger.vpweb.com
- Fertilizer—www.ahavenbrand.com
- Epiphytes—www.kkorchid.com

HELPFUL WEBSITES AND BLOGS

- www.plantsarethestrangestpeople.blogspot.com
- www.exoticangel.com
- www.davesgarden.com
- www.floridata.com
- www.gflora.com
- www.houseplantguru.blogspot.com
- www.debraleebaldwin.com

INDEX

MEET STEVE ASBELL

As a child growing up, Steve Asbell loved nature and chased lizards in the Mojave Desert. Before he became a passionate gardener, he was an avid hiker and could name just about every plant in the woods.

But when Steve Asbell's terminally ill mother started to lose her ability to see and walk as a result of lupus, he planted a garden in her Florida backyard and started a blog called The Rainforest Garden to share his uplifting experience, as well as his mother's extraordinary joy and gratitude. Now that she has passed away, he continues to garden for others and tends to the lush gardens that he planted for his neighbors in his apartment community.

Asbell's blog remains a respected source of inspiration for creative gardening DIY projects, and he now makes his living as a freelance writer, blogger, illustrator, and photographer. As a professional illustrator, he sees gardening as one of the most natural forms of art. You may have seen his work—his clients include Ferry-Morse (seed packets), Gardening Gone Wild, and Plants Nouveau. His illustrations have also been published on www.Southernliving.com, and his projects have been featured on Apartment Therapy, Mashable, and *Mother Earth News*.

Steve firmly believes that anyone can be an artist or gardener, if they are willing to learn. He lives with his wife, Jennifer, in Jacksonville, Florida. *Plant by Numbers* is Steve's first book, but not his last.